Nature
Swagger

Nature Swagger

RUE MAPP

Stories and Visions of Black Joy in the Outdoors

CHRONICLE BOOKS

SAN FRANCISCO

Library of Congress Cataloging-in-Publication Data

Names: Mapp, Rue, author.
Title: Nature swagger : visions of Black joy in the outdoors / Rue Mapp.
Description: San Francisco : Chronicle Books, [2022]
Identifiers: LCCN 2021059224 | ISBN 9781797214290 (Hardcover)
Subjects: LCSH: Outdoor recreation--Psychological aspects. | African Americans--Psychology--Miscellanea.
Classification: LCC GV191.6 .M3146 2022 | DDC 796.501/9--dc23/eng/20220201
LC record available at https://lccn.loc.gov/2021059224
ISBN: 978-1-7972-1429-0

Manufactured in China.

MIX
Paper | Supporting responsible forestry
FSC™ C008047
FSC
www.fsc.org

Design by Maggie Edelman.

10 9 8 7 6 5 4 3 2

Chronicle books and gifts are available at special quantity discounts to corporations, professional associations, literacy programs, and other organizations. For details and discount information, please contact our premiums department at corporatesales@chroniclebooks.com or at 1-800-759-0190.

Chronicle Books LLC
680 Second Street
San Francisco, California 94107
www.chroniclebooks.com

For Nathaniel and Reneé

Contents

Coming Home to Our Nature

By Shelton Johnson

When I was a boy growing up in Detroit back in the late '60s and early '70s, I was your typical inner-city kid, but I also harbored a secret passion. Yes, I sometimes played basketball or football with my neighborhood friends, but far more often I was buried in a book.

I didn't realize it at the time but I was trying to recapture a moment in time that not only profoundly shaped my past, but also determined my future. If not for that immersive experience when I was only five years old, I would not today be writing this narrative on behalf of Rue's book.

The family that I knew when I was a boy has all since passed away; my mother, father, and brother inhabit those memories of my boyhood and are very much alive in those recollections. I still see, hear, and feel their presence in a past where they will always live.

My father, James O. Johnson, Jr., served in both the U.S. Army and the Air Force, fought in the infantry in Korea, and served in the Air Force in Vietnam. We were not with him in war, but my family was together in peace. We lived in Germany and England when battlefields had become gardens and pastures again, and that stillness is the space I recall like a dream.

We were in London in 1964 when the Beatles were everywhere, and I clearly remember that energy, but what was stronger was also quieter. While my family lived in Contwig, Germany, in the

Rhineland-Palatinate, we took a trip to both the Black Forest and to Berchtesgaden in the Bavarian Alps.

These beautiful environments were the locale of my baptism into nature, my spiritual awakening into the world. The Black Forest was the doorway that led to the sacred immersion we call a forest, and Berchtesgaden was that ascent to those astonishing heights we call mountains.

Imagine the impact on the psyche of a little boy to be introduced to such a world and then spend the rest of his childhood mostly in Detroit when it had the highest homicide rate in the country.

There, I lived next door to the parents of Norman Whitfield, who wrote "Papa was a Rollin' Stone" and "I Heard It through the Grapevine" for Motown Records. There, I learned how to survive the streets. There, the memories of that time overseas not only did not fade, but they deepened such that it was inevitable that I would one day become a National Park Ranger.

Germany was deeper than Black joy in the great outdoors. It was a profound awakening, a forge that fired my mind, imagination, and spirit, an immersion that turned my first visit to Yellowstone in 1984 into a homecoming. When a Black kid born and raised in Detroit feels that traveling to Montana and Wyoming is going home, well, that says everything about why Black people need to engage with our national parks, forests, lakeshores, seashores, and wild and scenic rivers.

We all descend from Native people, from African people, and those blood memories are barely beneath the surface of our people. Just a walk through a grove of giant sequoia in Yosemite, a geyser basin in Yellowstone, or to any mountaintop in America generates enough friction to burn off that thin veneer of the city and reveal the country within all of us, and I don't mean Mississippi or Georgia, I mean Mali or Ghana.

The African within all of us is just waiting for the opportunity to walk, discover, and explore again. Give her or him that moment of spirit, of grace, to awaken our bodies, minds, and souls to the joy of being Indigenous again, children again, exploring wild new worlds.

—Shelton Johnson

A Standing Invitation

Rue Mapp

Our family's ranch in Lake County, California, stood on fourteen acres of land covered in English walnut trees and sprawling oak trees that shaded our modest home. The entrance to our driveway was flanked by a rock masonry frame, and hanging from it was a homemade black-and white-sign with letters carved out by a wood router: Big Oak. It was a remarkable corner lot, with open ranch fencing on two sides that allowed anyone driving by to easily take in what was going on in the yard. People routinely slowed as they rounded the corner to see what lively events were happening at Big Oak.

The land was lovingly and purposely tended to by my father, A. C. Levias, who delighted in creating both its form and function to enhance the experience for our biweekly family runs, and for everyone who frequently visited our ranch. There was a barn and a shop, built with symbiotic purposes in mind. These would be where we built the pen that housed our pigs and other livestock. Beyond that lay a bountiful vegetable garden. Vines full of grapes and trees heavy with fruit in the summer. My father also built a walk-in smokehouse, a swimming pool, a swing set, and eventually a tennis court. Altogether, our ranch was a place that holistically embodied outdoorsman grit, with a nod to community entertainment and a resort-style twang.

My dad was a Black man from the Jim Crow South with an eighth-grade education who had the audacity to create a place like this in a nearly all-white town. But he was respected in the community, and on one occasion, the county newspaper covered one of our large family events on its front page.

As a child, I was always thrilled to visit the ranch. I delighted in taking part in hunting, fishing, and exploring the surrounding woodlands along country roads by foot or on my bike. Nearby Copsey Creek was an oasis of discovery and learning about aquatic ecosystems as well as the seasonal flow of water. I recall many times getting out of the car and wondering if those tadpoles—or pollywogs—I saw a couple of weeks before had turned into frogs. How high was the river after the big rain?

At the ranch, I fell deeply in love with nature.

More than just bountiful and beautiful land, the ranch was also a site for celebration, where we invited family, friends, and members of the community to enjoy holidays, parties, and reunions. I especially loved when we kids put together talent shows for the adults, who would spend the day talking, laughing, and playing games like bid whist and dominoes.

I received lessons in hospitality at the ranch. My dad had a famous saying, "You have a *standing invitation*," meaning, once you have visited our home,

you are always welcome back. Sometimes there would be so many people dropping by or staying over, it felt like the house might explode. But there was always enough room for everyone, even if it meant people slept on the kitchen floor with a homemade quilt or under a makeshift sheet tent outside. And there was *always* something cooking or ready on the stove, on the grill, or right out of the oven—one more barbecued rib, a bowl of collard greens, a slice of 7-Up cake, a cup of punch. Nothing lacking. The hospitality my parents showed everyone is still unsurpassed and still raved about to this day.

Those welcoming ways of the ranch meant that adults and children alike could experience wonder under the bright stars at night (unseen back

home in a light-polluted cityscape). Air so fresh and fragrant of lake and oak woodlands. The euphoric sound and experience of silence. I had a front-row seat to the joy of community in that nature, which brought about in me a yearning to create and be a part of something like it for the rest of my life.

Back home in Oakland, I participated in Girl Scouts, which reminded me of the intimacy and affinity of the community on my family ranch. I loved the Girl Scout mottos, our songs, and our rituals, but the highlight was learning how to camp. Mind you, my family had been an outdoor-loving family, but no one saw the need or had the wherewithal to camp. That might have been regarded as something other people do. After my first experience with my Girl Scout troop, I was hooked on camping and everything it encompassed; even chores were more fun tackled as a group in nature, while singing songs.

It was at this same time that I started a diary, a prized Hello Kitty red padded book with empty lines of possibility. In those pages, I was especially drawn to capturing my time in nature. In painstaking detail, through my new curly cursive, I wrote what I saw and what I did, and shared the stories of how we related to one another in our pop-up community.

Around this same time, I became fascinated by technology. Growing up in the Bay Area meant being exposed to the cutting edge of early computer technology. Carl B. Munck, my Oakland public elementary school, had Commodore PET computers for our classroom. By the age of ten, I was programming BASIC language so easily that my parents purchased a home version of the Commodore for me so I could continue to practice this new skill and passion. I would sometimes bring my computer to the ranch and practice programming in quieter moments.

I eventually found my passion for activism and community service in college through both the Black Student Union, and Women's Center, where I would make lifelong friends. By the early '90s I had a capstone experience mountaineering with Outward Bound and summited peaks in the high Sierra as the only Black woman in our group. That trip summed up an acute awareness in me to understand nature as a powerful teacher, while also highlighting the isolation I felt as a young Black woman still trying to navigate young adulthood in a new, remote wilderness setting with people who shared cultural experiences different from my own.

Out of my experience using digital technology over the years, it was easy to become an early adopter of the internet. And with a renewed focus on the outdoors as a young adult, I sought out other outdoor enthusiast discussion groups in the World Wide Web's Usenet. But my in-person group experiences that came out of those discussions were not satisfying. I did not feel welcomed, nor understood for my abilities. Group organizers did not always explain what I needed to know to have a successful, fun, and safer experience. And far too often, I did not experience groups of people with more folks who looked like me.

With a lifetime of understanding nature and community under my feet, I knew how I benefited greatly from it all along. As I became a wife and mother, nature was a solid place to nurture my family, and an affordable way to experience vacation, visiting local beaches and trails discovered in travel books, often close to home. We became regulars at our city's affordable family camp, where it was easy to make friends, as we spent hours under the trees talking, watching talent show performances, and indulging in all the eating we could at its Chow Palace. But still, in having these experiences, especially farthest away from Oakland, I saw few Black people, and felt like my community was missing out on all that I knew nature had given me.

In my early thirties, my life changed dramatically. I was no longer married, and was raising three children on my own. I decided to return to college to tend to a long-neglected undergraduate degree, understanding the need to have more options to earn a living and support my family. After two years of sleepless nights of study at a junior college, while working full time with determination, I found relief in an admission letter to UC Berkeley. For the next three years, me and my kids went to college (though only one of us was sitting in its classrooms).

But toward the end of my degree completion, I was looking over the edge into a country in recession. The goal of getting that great job did not seem certain anymore. So I considered business school, and found support from a mentor to explore that option, but that, too, was going to be a challenge. How could I consider going away from my community to study intensely with my three growing children who needed me more than ever?

I'll never forget the moment in a conversation with that mentor, Freada Kapor Klien, who understood my dilemma and asked, "If time and money were not an issue, what would you do?"

I opened my mouth, and my life fell out.

"I'd probably start a website to reconnect Black people to the outdoors."

It was a moment of revelation, a key that fit perfectly into the lock of this magic moment, opening the door to possibilities that are still unfolding. It was as if the truths of my life were hiding in plain sight and now wanted to be seen and understood.

Community, nature, technology, and writing could be finally woven into a single expression. It was a moment of a true homecoming for me, to be fully expressed and healed as an individual, while providing a chance to help my community do the same.

Soon after that talk with Freada, I pulled out my laptop and created a new blog, which I quickly yet thoughtfully named *Outdoor Afro*, using a borrowed template and a photo of me on a mountain in California's Sierra, on that transformative Outward Bound trip. My first blog post was titled "How Did an Oakland Girl Like Me Come to Love Getting Her Camp On Anyway?" and I told the story of growing up in a family that loved both nature and community, describing how it was possible for an Oakland girl to come to love nature, and how those experiences helped me to learn, grow, and appreciate myself and others. The comments were overwhelmingly supportive: "I'm so glad I found you," "I'd love to camp with you sometime," or "I feel like you made this blog for me."

It was not long before I received encouraging reactions from people from all over the United States, who reflected back to me their own joy and love in nature. Something was resonating. I had recently studied art history at UC Berkeley and understood the discipline and power of representation to tell stories, along with the importance of using current technologies to share that representation at scale. I reflected on my studies about Sojourner Truth's *carte de visite*, or calling cards, that leveraged the new technology of photography during the Civil War to create greater visibility for the movement that successfully abolished slavery and ended a war. Now before me in 2009 was a new frontier of social media that democratized and forever changed how public relations and marketing could work. From my kitchen table I decided to tell a new story using images—unlike anything I had seen growing up among the glossy outdoor and nature publications—of Black people in nature as strong, beautiful, and free. Just like what I always knew and experienced growing up.

Over the following years I gave myself over to my work with increasing focus and determination. I took a part-time job at my local Audubon, where I learned about environmental conservation, and later at a foundation that helped me to understand how Outdoor Afro might fit into a field of work. I leveraged my years of personal and professional networking and experiences in business, the arts, and community building to level up that blog to become a national and staffed organization that today broadens the definition of not only what outdoor participation looks like, but also who leads these experiences.

In the past twelve years since I sat down and wrote that first blog post, Outdoor Afro has grown into an organization that touches thousands through in-person adventure, and millions more through digital media to broaden what outdoor participation looks like and who leads experiences in nature all over the country. You'll find Outdoor Afro leaders getting people out to camp in the Colorado Rockies, hike in view of the St. Louis Gateway Arch, bird-watch in the Florida Everglades, canoe in the Mississippi River, and more—all while learning about the long heritage of Black people connecting in nature. Some of our trained leaders have even gone on to do capstone events together, such as climb the Sierra heights of

Mount Whitney in California, walk in Harriet Tubman's footsteps along the Appalachian trail, and pilgrimage to the far reaches of Africa in Tanzania to find new definitions of *summit* on Mount Kilimanjaro, surrounded by people who look like them.

This journey has taken me to many different places and introduced me to many incredible people who have become my newest wave of lifelong friends, all of which has taught me profound lessons about the personal and societal challenges that nature is adept at helping us solve. In the years of racial divide and civic unrest in which my work developed, we began Healing Hikes as a showcase of continued and expanded clarity of the power of nature to teach, transform, and heal. We can also lift up and expand on beloved historical figures such as Harriet Tubman as a true wilderness leader. She absolutely journeyed our people to freedom through nature. Most importantly, it's become clearer to me over the years that nature is not some place over *there*—it is present within us. Always. Therefore, the concept of connecting people to nature is actually a journey inward and a homecoming with oneself.

As I joyously learned about nature and myself over the years, I eventually felt the quickening of a book that wanted to be born so I could share the gift of our empowered story with others. I felt transported to the innocent, yet powerful, moment when I wrote in a journal for the first time as a child, and understood there was so much more I needed to write about and share today—not only my own journey to become joyously transformed through nature, but also the stories of others who might never have had the specific and loving platform of this book. A diary all grown up.

While enthusiastically focused on Black American experiences, *Nature Swagger* is a universal roadmap to discover the delights, joys, and possibilities of transformation for *anyone* through nature. You will discover the epiphanies of high adventure alongside meditations on love of a favorite place or person, and poetic revelations about our wild foodways—how it can all work together, and, by extension, how we can, too.

This book, as my father would describe it, is your standing invitation to reconnect with nature, and write your own story and transform within it.

Homecoming

Reunions in Nature

For many Black Americans, the phrases *homecoming* and *family reunion* are interchangeable and can exist one inside the other. And for many who shared their stories in this book, the concepts of homecoming and reunion in nature are recurrent. As humans and animals, we easily turn to nature to find something that was either lost or wants to be found.

For newly emancipated slaves, family reunions were a lifeline and a network to help people find relatives lost in the disruptive system of enslavement, as well as a way to create new kinship bonds. Decades later, as the great migration brought up to six million Black people from the South to the last stop of train stations in America's north, east, and west, the reunion became even more critical to maintain family bonds, traditions, and unity. Reunions often include scores of relatives of all ages, sometimes hundreds, who gather in a span of a few summer days of jam-packed activities that can include storytelling, games, outdoor activities, performances, visiting historic family sites, church services, and recognition of graduations and other family milestones, and through

it all, mountains of delicious family recipes prepared by loving hands, and plenty of knee-slapping expressions of joy.

Family—of origin or choice—is where we belong. And we already belong to nature—we are nature. In my work over the years, when asked questions like "Why are Black people not connected to nature?" I always respond that we have *always* had a connection. While nature for some might mean traveling to a distant destination or adventuring through peak experiences, I enjoy reminding people of their family practices and personal connections to nature, such as a grandmother's backyard garden, or fishing in a nearby lake with an uncle, or the childlike glee of splashing in wet, muddy puddles after a good rain. Nature even resides within us—it is the water that makes up the largest percentage of the Earth and of our body mass that leaves little wonder how lunar cycles affect not only the tides, but also our moods. It is the air we breathe. Nature is always at hand.

In nature there is often a curious tension between foreign and familiar. As humans we tend to seek a reflection of our own image. In family reunions there is a mix of both fondness and belonging in a recognized familiar facial feature, a common expression of form, or an accent. But sometimes those connections are not easily seen, and are discovered instead through a shared origin story around the embers of a campfire, or when spirit hits in a moment when a particular verse of a hymn is sung.

My first official family reunion experience was organized at a local park in the Oakland Hills, in a grass clearing with orderly, lined picnic tables between the shade and scent of redwoods, bay laurels, and oaks. It was as beautiful as it was convenient, a spacious way for the broader clan to come together from far and wide, bearing and sharing heavy platters and trays of meats, salads, and sweet treats. Like my mom's famous sweet potato pie, or Uncle Clarence's caught and fried catfish. Generations of the Levias family, the family of my origin, and the intersecting Farr family line had roots and stories that went back to an enslaved American past. Leviases came from far and wide, from Seattle and Los Angeles, where many landed in our great migration, and a hearty number took on the two-day drive from down home (East Texas or Louisiana) every few years for occasions like this one.

Over the years, as my family's branch has been fractured and dispersed through

death, divorce, and land loss, the feeling of yearning for home and family connections has only intensified for me. As my professional work became rooted in the familiarity of nature, it felt easy and natural to create a new kind of kinship with people who shared outdoor experiences. When I decided to become a local outdoor recreation leader, I took elements of hospitality I learned from my family, lessons as a participant in groups and clubs over the years, and innovations from my new park ranger and interpreter friends. The experience of gathering other people—especially people who looked like me—was refreshing and inspiring. Familiar, comforting, and celebratory—like a homecoming.

In leading events, I've learned that welcoming is not just about words or gestures of outreach. It is about relationships. It's about making people feel that sense of belonging. I decided to begin every event I hosted with an opening circle, so that people could not only introduce themselves individually to the group—their name and hometown—but also share what they already loved being or doing in nature. It was important to ground people in an empowered and familiar view of who they already are in nature, as opposed to a false

assumption that they had no connection—or, worse, did not belong.

"I'm Candice, and I'm from Santa Cruz, and I love the beach. . . ."

"I'm Otis, I'm from Oakland, and I love cookouts. . . ."

"I'm Tamela, I'm new in town from Austin, Texas, and I like camping under the stars. . . ."

Each time we shared, we made a community.

These experiences inspired me to build a team of leaders, learners, and sharers of that community connection, and replicate all I learned so that it could be shared with more people around the country.

In 2013, I turned to the Internet once again and asked, "Who wants to be an Outdoor Afro leader?"

More than a dozen folks from around the country answered the call and became part of the inaugural Outdoor Afro Leadership Team. These men and women represented a breadth of regions and talents, the perfect mix needed to help people connect to their unique local nature and communities. At our first training, we gathered together

> "When I attend their events as a participant, I see how people come together initially as strangers in those opening circles, but leave with a feeling of being part of a family, sharing prayer-like words such as *peace, healing, love,* and *gratitude.*"

in the mountains of Lake County around a campfire, overlooking the majestic and familiar Clear Lake, where I had learned to love the outdoors in so many ways. We discovered the significance of telling our stories in nature, the value in noticing our connection to it, and, importantly, how to help people feel safer and comforted by it.

Today the experience of that team has grown to include hundreds of leaders we have trained over the years, and they touch the lives of millions of people, both in person and online. What they have ultimately become is a network of welcoming and hospitality, what I affectionately refer to as a pop-up family reunion. When I attend events as a participant, I see how people come together initially as strangers in those opening circles, but leave with a feeling of being part of a family,

sharing prayer-like words such as *peace, healing, love,* and *gratitude.* A group that started as strangers become grounded in the circles and create a bond that will continue to expand into their weeks, days, homes, and workplaces, a reminder that nature is about belonging and creating a home for everyone.

I experience with all participants the elements I've learned: the feelings of connection through a compelling invitation, and that familiar ranch-style hospitality that also creates a sense of family and belonging.

A homecoming among kin.

—Rue

Family Unity

Robin Brumfield-Johnson

Going to the ranch near Clearlake, California, with my family was the happiest part of my childhood. There were so many things we could do at that ranch that we could not do at home on Burr Street, the narrow street in Oakland where we grew up.

Summertime in Clearlake for us kids was about fruit-picking in the morning and swimming all afternoon. We made costumes before we got to Clearlake for the talent shows we produced for the family. And once we were all together at the ranch, we scripted and practiced our routines.

We also learned how to be independent during these visits. We could walk a mile down the road to the store, and visit the creek by ourselves as young kids. We learned to cook and eat foods we never had before—like cornbread and fresh fish. We'd see the fish caught, then cut up and breaded with cornmeal, and fried that night for dinner—all on the same day. These things just didn't happen in Oakland, California.

I loved to observe deer and rabbits on our drive up on the road to the ranch. If it weren't for Clearlake, I probably never would have tasted venison, or had deer jerky made at the local Pomo tribe's reservation. Sometimes if our fathers didn't go out on the boat, they would also buy fish from the reservation. I was recently telling my daughter about how on the reservation they would catch fish, put them in an empty milk carton, fill it with water, and freeze it, and then we would buy it.

For my dad, going to that ranch must have felt akin to his own upbringing in McComb, Mississippi—starting our days before dawn, sitting out on the porch, reminiscing and visiting all day—though I don't think he saw it as exciting as we did. But I think it brought up good memories for him. They even served us Kool-Aid punch recipes from the South that were ladled out of white buckets. Oh, my goodness. I think that's funny now, but it was part of our culture, and I know that my parents knew how happy it made us to experience these things. It was a treat for us, and whenever we learned we were going to Clearlake we would scream and jump up and down with excitement. I know now just how it made my parents feel because I know how excited I am when I do something for my kids that they love. But I think my parents also found their peace of mind, as they were always made to feel like they were at home.

I'll always remember the family unity, which was just so beautiful. When I look at the different families that came together on that ranch, all the different ages, each had their part to play—everyone took part in either cooking or chores. I especially enjoyed the storytelling. Today, when families get together, sometimes people split up and go to a separate room to watch the game or play video games, and others hang out in the kitchen, with the kids outside. At Clearlake, everybody was together all the time, having fun. I still share with my daughters stories about that kind of family unity. And while I do keep unity alive with my sisters, those were different times that were about a whole community that also included neighbors and friends. I'll always hold dear those joyous times in nature the ranch gave us all.

Robin Brumfield Johnson, and the author's family were close, lifelong friends. Some of her greatest childhood memories are from days spent outdoors at a ranch in Clearlake, California, and she enjoys sharing those stories with her children and grandchildren. She lives in Oakland, California.

My Summit

Leandra Taylor

Climbing Kilimanjaro, the highest peak in Africa, changed and shaped me as a person. It taught me how to take care of myself, find support in teammates, and push past my own perceived limits.

On day four of my journey up the mountain, I faced one of my biggest fears: my fear of heights. Halfway through the day's hike, I started having a panic attack. As we hiked higher and higher, I tried to stay in my body, and kept telling myself, "I am strong, my body is strong, my legs are strong." I had one of the guides hold my hand. That small gesture, literally holding my hand with all of his strength, was so intimate. It was something that I saw happen on the mountain several times. I watched our expedition leader and other Black men hold one another, hold their hands with an intimacy we don't often see here in the United States.

When we finally made it to our campsite that day, I had the shakes. My brain was as tired as it could be. My legs felt like noodles. I collapsed in my tent and I ended up getting sick.

One of my teammates came by and said, "This is okay, this is fine, you're fine. Just come join us for dinner." I was so embarrassed because this was my first time throwing up on a trail—I had a lot of firsts that day! Once I dragged myself to the meal, our guide said, "You just need to eat dinner, drink water, go to sleep, and stop thinking." And those four things that he

said to me changed the way that I perceive the limits I place on myself and the way that I take care of myself when I'm at that point. I get chills thinking about that revelation now. *Eat, drink water, sleep, stop thinking.* Indeed, I ended up simply getting in my tent and lying down after our meal. I remember lying there thinking, "I'm not done climbing." I knew the next day was the Barranco Wall, which is even higher than what we did that day.

I'm not done climbing.

I woke up that next day feeling transformed. The sleeping bag had been my cocoon and I woke up a brand-new butterfly. And I still had my teammates next to me, showing me what support can look like in life: how to ask for it, how to receive it, and how to give it to myself. I don't think I've ever given myself that kind of grace—the grace of saying *It's okay to rest, it's okay to say you're tired, it's okay to say you need support from other people* when you're exhausted and depleted. That day I woke up feeling brand new and understood that only I was the one placing the limits on my life, on the things that I can do.

This was the day that I summited in my spirit, an emotional and new elevation and enlightenment. I did make it to the geographic summit later, but this was *my* summit date. This was the day that I grew stronger. I realized all the different things that I carry within myself, my power, and the things that you can do when you have true support. This was a powerful moment of reflection for me. It was a life-changing day and a life-changing sleep. I woke up feeling changed, unlike I've ever felt before.

Before that trip I felt really lost about where I was in my life. After the expedition, once I left that mountain, I realized I was finally in tune and in touch with who I am and who I'm supposed to be. I think about it every day of my life.

Leandra Taylor is an artist and Outdoor Afro leader. She lives in Asheville, North Carolina.

Unapologetic in Nature

Julius Crowe Hampton

My Black joy means to be in my full Black essence. Unapologetically and unafraid.

When I think about being unapologetic and unafraid in nature, I'm at home with my mind, with my body, with my spirit. I am in tune with my surroundings, getting strength from my surroundings, getting strength from the redwood trees, tapping in to their ancestral strength. Ultimately, I feel alive and whole and I'm where I need to be. I am a beacon of Black light.

I love to experience nature in many different ways. I love solo hike expeditions and also experiencing nature with my husband, Abram. We've had several transformative adventures together, especially in the water. I am a full-time elementary school teacher, and I love experiencing nature with children and seeing them in their freedom and glory. My journeys in nature with Outdoor Afro have all been profound experiences of Black people coming together to cultivate healing, community, and joy. It is rare to experience all of that in our society, which is why I keep coming back.

I've especially turned to redwoods during both challenging and joyous times. One time that comes to mind is when I was coming out to my family. It was scary. I definitely spent a lot of meditative time in nature to develop

the emotional balance and strength I needed to tackle the challenge. I knew the redwoods have been through a lot—they're bold and resilient. I needed all of that energy. So whenever I would go to the redwoods, I would tap in to that. I also noticed a creek that goes through the redwoods, which for me was a metaphor for the flexibility and also the impermanence of nature. It was a reminder that even though a situation feels hard right now, I am capable of getting through hard times.

I want to continue to both challenge myself and grow in nature. For instance, I grew up afraid of large bodies of water. So recently, I have been trying to heal from that by paddle-boarding and kayaking in the local bay. In these experiences, it has felt extremely liberating to step away from fear and be at peace on the water. I hold so much reverence for water for all of the lessons it has to share. My time paddling on the water reminds me to live my life with passion and not with fear.

Nature needs to be cared for deeply and it needs to be protected—it's so precious and fragile. I want everyone to feel connected and to see themselves in nature so that they can take really good care of it. Mama Nature needs all of the love, respect, care, and protection she can get these days.

Julius Crowe Hampton is a fourth-grade teacher in Oakland, California. He loves to spend time in the redwoods.

Quiet Strength

Yanira M. Castro

My grandfather was a carpenter, and his homeland was Puerto Rico. Like many fathers and mothers, he immigrated to the United States to forge a new life for his growing family. My maternal grandparents were both very instrumental in my life, but my grandfather Teodoro would vacation with us to Puerto Rico regularly.

When I was eight years old, he took me to El Yunque National Rainforest, and I had my very first transformative nature experience. I remember him, machete in hand, making a way out of no way. There were no trails or markers to guide us. No map or GPS, just the knowledge of his homeland, his ancestral place. I don't know how long we hiked, but I do remember exiting the brush into the clouds. There was no view, just mist and fog and moisture. We never did see the view that day, but I don't believe I have ever felt closer to God, standing with my *abuelo*, listening to his breath and being empowered by his quiet strength.

Thirty years later, I was stuck in an unfulfilling job, where I knew my craft in communications well, and I was stifling. I eventually decided to quit and take the chance to start my own communications business. Over two years, I traveled the world with my children, always seeking outdoor adventures. I did things I had never done before, and I built a life anchored in the truth of my strengths and desires. Nature was the conduit for all of it, and it was always right there waiting for me. I just needed to give myself permission to embrace it.

My grandfather was the first to do that for me, but somewhere along the way, that passion faded away. Maybe I felt a lack of safety, a common feeling among Black and Brown women, not only outdoors, but in life. Maybe it was my drive to succeed and not feeling I had the right or the time for frivolous things. Maybe it was that I never saw someone that looked like me empowered in outdoor experiences.

I now can only imagine what the rest of my life holds. My desire is to inspire with my stories, to bring others along, and to share that things aren't that far out of your reach if you just look.

Yanira Castro is a world traveler, and the founder and CEO of Humanity Communications, a boutique social justice-centered communications firm. She resides in North Carolina with her husband and children.

Black Horseman

Virgil Baker

I first got into riding horses when I was living in Uganda and working as a volunteer there. I was sharing a house with another volunteer named Gordon, who was from Texas. One day Gordon brought a racehorse back to our shared house and showed us the basics of horseback riding.

After four years in Africa, I went back to the States, and eventually I found a group of riders in the Bay Area. My daughter and I became more involved with riding.

Long story short, I ended up buying a couple of horses.

The group we rode with was connected to other Black horsemen who had been riding in the Bay Area for years. Many of the horsemen came from the South and settled in San Francisco. There used to be a barn in Richmond, California, run by JJ and Melvin, originally from Louisiana, that provided affordable horse boarding, charging something like seventy-five bucks a month. But you had to clean your own stall and bring your own feed. They ended up with few hundred horses out that way, but eventually they needed more space and had to move near a landfill. Then the landfill took over the property and they ended up finding another piece of land in the Central Valley.

We rode in a mixed group of mainly Black riders, some white riders, and several Mexican American riders. Our group used to get together with other riding groups on weekends and do campouts. Friday night we had a fish fry. And then Saturday was usually the big riding day. After the ride we would bring out the music and dance and play cards and have a good time. It was a pretty fun time for folks to get together.

On Sundays we often had pastors and ministers who would do a sermon in the morning and then we'd have a community breakfast. Everybody put the breakfast stuff together. And then, those who didn't have other things to do, like get home to watch football, would ride again on Sundays.

During the riding season we rode at least a couple of times a month at various state, regional, and national parks. It became popular, and we used to have events that would attract as many as eighty people. We would also bring in entertainment—sometimes Black country and western singers or R & B singers. My daughter would go to these events with me—they were very family oriented, with a lot of the kids growing up together in that world.

We had a lot of people involved at one point, but eventually, many of the folks, particularly the younger ones, began to take more of an interest in their friends. Some people got different jobs, and they were busy. It got to a point where it was just a few of the old-timers hanging on, still doing what we had been doing, getting together for weekends, but a little less frequently.

But a few years ago, some of the riding groups started to grow again. There was one group that created a program that got kids off the streets and taught them riding at a ranch just east of Stockton. They also used to come out and camp with us.

Now a lot of young riders have come into the fold, and new adult riders have come in, too. And so the old-timers have a new crowd of people who we hang out with. A couple of months ago we had 400 participants! Horse riding is coming back stronger than ever. I love it.

Virgil Baker, a retired civil engineer and former entrepreneur, is a horseman and an outdoorsman and avid trail rider. He has ridden trails throughout California, from the desert to the Pacific Ocean, from mountain trails to flatland roads. He resides in California's Contra Costa County.

Everyday Family Nature

Pandora Thomas

My father, Lawrence "Jelly" Thomas (now an ancestor), and my mom, Frances, raised us in a small steel town in Pennsylvania with a population of 6,000 people.

My parents loved Cadillacs, and our whole family—my mom, dad, sister, and I—would pile in one every weekend, and take our drives out to go to a place called Under the Bridge. I remember us being the cutest Black family, with our little afros, always wearing stylish clothing like bell bottoms.

I learned from my family to celebrate nature in our own way every day. We were a church-bound family, and went to church every Sunday. I also grew up attending Catholic school. Our family was rooted in the idea that God and spirituality were also nature. Our tiny house was filled with indoor plants and it was gorgeous, like a showroom. My mom breezed around the house, rotating her plants inside and out through the seasons. She had the greenest thumb. She still does.

My dad was an avid fisherman, and he would take our family to Pymatuning Reservoir, a man-made lake in Crawford County, to go fishing. People would feed guppies bread and then the ducks would come and walk on top of the fish. Who knows the ecological consequences of that, but that we were all out there as a family enjoying the outdoors together seemed most important.

I visited that reservoir recently and I thought, *Oh, my gosh!* I can't believe that after forty-five years, the place hadn't changed. I could still picture the scene where my dad would be fishing, my mom would be reading, and I would be playing with rocks.

My father also taught me to love worms. He would use worms or minnows as bait for fishing, and he kept a whole box of worms in our basement—I spent time down there playing with the worms and giving them names. He taught me about the biology of worms and how to use them as bait for the fish. Several years ago, before moving to a new farm, I dreamt I was an earthworm, and it took me back to memories of my dad teaching me about worms. Perhaps he wanted to be an encouraging presence in this big moment.

These early experiences planted the seeds that eventually led me to become an environmental educator and farmer. After many years of hard work, incredible support, and dreaming big, I founded the EARTHseed Permaculture Center and Farm, a place where thousands of adults and youth annually reclaim their relationship to the Earth, their history, and their future through learning about Afro-Indigenous permaculture. Black-led and operated, it serves as a working farm and retreat and educational center to allow respite and Earth-centered relaxation, while also reconnecting communities to sustainable practices for living healthily in our world today.

I've come to appreciate how connections to nature show up easily in our lives. It is our breath, our knowledge that we're not separate: we are nature working, we are an animal, we are part of a system. I really feel that my parents taught me that just by who they were, their belief in God, and a spirit that was about connecting everything.

I also believe that they got that from our African ancestry—that unbridled present connection, which is still in our communities. It's who we are. No one can take that away. And that is a core part of EARTHseed. It's creating a sense of place among the 4,000 trees that grow around the farm. This land called us. We answered the call to take this ease of connection to nature to the next level. At this farm we get to live our story. I feel it has been so well stewarded and appointed for this moment, where Black folks can have a place to go and create the same beautiful Blackness in nature that my family stepped into every day. I'm honored.

Pandora Thomas is the founder of EARTHseed Permaculture Center and Farm, a fourteen-acre solar-powered organic farm and orchard located in scenic Sonoma County, California. The farm is operated and rooted in Afro-Indigenous permaculture principles and built on the long legacy of Earth wisdom traditions of people of African descent.

The Outdoors as a Lifestyle

Phil Henderson

Black joy and nature didn't go hand in hand for me until I visited Kenya in 2000 with other Black outdoor trip leaders. That is really when I felt acknowledged and recognized by people. I had never worked with another Black person in the outdoors, so that experience was a big switch and an emotional high as I discovered what had been missing in my outdoor life: to be seen and understood.

Black people see things differently. We recreate differently. We relax differently. And it was like a lightbulb went on: okay, this is what I've been wanting to experience and what I realized was missing. There was something about slowing down, relaxing, and enjoying being in nature versus a constant "go, go, go!" culture. It also felt good to be acknowledged for my experiences and skills.

One reason why I have such a connection with East Africa's people, and especially those who work outdoors, is because if you live, recreate, and work in the United States, and have never gone to Africa, you wouldn't think that Black people work outdoors on a large scale. I mean, for example, if you go to a national park, how many dark-skinned rangers do you see there? In Kenya, I saw all the Black park rangers, and it made me feel like I

wanted to wear *that* uniform, you know? I never felt like I could be a part of parks in this way.

But I had always known that I wanted to provide joy in nature for Black people. As a child I learned to fish. I would go fishing before baseball games, and I would want to take my friends with me. When I wanted to go hiking, it was the same. I've always been that way—I wanted to create what I was feeling in nature for others. Sometimes people thought I was crazy and asked, "Why would you do *that*?" But I always had that drive to share because I knew there's something inside of everyone that can get connected to nature. You just have to find the right thing at the right time.

Black joy to me is global, and that's one of the reasons why the Kilimanjaro trip with Black outdoor leaders was very important to me—it meant connecting with our African culture and connecting with the outdoors as Black people. All the porters who brought us food so we could stay on the mountain were Black, as well as the other staff. The mutual respect we experienced with all those people was remarkable.

It was also illuminating to see how people in East Africa are connected to working in the outdoors to provide for their families, while also living in outdoor settings; they are much more connected to the natural environment. For me that connection means I enjoy gardening as much as I enjoy climbing. It's not a job, it's a lifestyle. It's how I feed my family, and while I might go to the mountain for work, when I come home, I'm still digging in the dirt to grow vegetables and flowers.

The outdoors is a lifestyle and it's one that I want other people to discover. Because I wanted to work in the outdoor industry, I moved to a small town in the Colorado Rockies; as a result, I also benefit from breathing cleaner air, I have the ability to grow my own garden, and I own land and animals that altogether enhance my life. While not everybody can have that, there's still a possibility for people to grow their own food even if they live in the city. There's still the possibility of going to a park and taking a walk and relaxing and having the outdoors be a part of your lifestyle.

And now there are even more opportunities to earn a living in this field— such as in climbing gyms and summer camps. So it brings me joy to see broader opportunities than I saw in the outdoor industry of the '90s. There are more Black people, not only enjoying and recreating in the outdoors, but also working outdoors and having an outdoor lifestyle. More Black people are moving from the larger cities into smaller towns, and that's what it's going to take for us to really make an impact. Black people are not just a sidebar of the outdoor industry. We are part of the mainstream, but it's going to take more of us to show up and create this lifestyle for ourselves. Working in the outdoor industry is a big part of my life, and my lifestyle is being outside. It's what brings me joy.

Phil Henderson lives in the Colorado Rockies with his wife and daughter. He is renowned for his experiential mountaineering leadership, and especially enjoys exploration in East Africa and in his backyard garden.

Reclaiming My Black Joy in Nature

Alison Rose Jefferson, MHC, PhD

My enjoyment of nature and the outdoors developed early in my life, as I crisscrossed the Los Angeles region's diverse and layered urban, natural, geographic, topographic, and cultural landscapes. I liked being outside, feeling the sunshine's warmth on my skin as I explored and learned from the places my family and family friends lived, and other places I visited with them. My joy in the outdoors has always been about my day-to-day living; I have an experience in "nature" wherever I am. Except for visits to ocean beaches, my experiences going to what would be considered "wild nature places," like a national park or a wilderness area, have been few.

I grew up in Los Angeles in the 1960s, and my mom, Marcelyn, used to take me and my younger brother, Albert Jr., to the beach, where we would enjoy the caress of the sun, wind, sand, and salty ocean water. My mom was a Los Angeles Unified School District teacher, and she had summer vacations off with us. During those summers, she made sure we learned how to swim well, as she viewed swimming as a life skill that should be part of everyone's education. She took me and my brother to swimming lessons at the private Waikiki Swim School not far from our home, which was owned by an ethnic Hawaiian family. To this day I appreciate that the Hawaiian teachers helped me, their little Black girl pupil, overcome my fear of swimming in pool-deep

water. Their teaching and this accomplishment helped my confidence in other areas of my life.

Our oceanfront day adventures were at Will Rogers State Beach on the Pacific Coast Highway. My mom would sometimes allow me and my brother to each bring a playmate with us. Sometimes we made friends for the day if they were near where my mother positioned our shoreline temporary encampment. I do not remember seeing other African American people at this beach.

I later realized my mom probably liked this beach paralleling the northern Pacific Palisades area because it was never too crowded with people. She would drive us there before noon so she could park the car in one of the few spaces of a small lot or on the street. Mom could relax on the warm sand and enjoy getting in the cool Pacific Ocean while keeping her eyes on us.

I loved bodysurfing and belly-boarding. In addition to the fun of floating and playing in the ocean, I felt a sense of accomplishment when I figured out the right waves to catch that I could ride before they crashed into white water foam. Sometimes my brother and I would dig in the wet shoreline sand to see who could find the largest sand crabs. A few times we tried to bring the sand crabs home in a plastic bucket with water and sand so we could take them to school for show-and-tell. Mom nixed this idea, as she made us leave our catch, explaining to us that the sand crabs needed the ocean coastal zone to live and that they would not survive at our house.

I never thought much about our family's beach adventures as being something that many other African American families might not have had easy access to. As a little Black girl I was aware of these injustices, as the adults in my life talked about them and because I saw the 1960s civil rights protests and Watts Uprising presented in newspapers, magazines, and on TV. When we went to the Will Rogers State Beach, I imagine my mom, in seizing our family's collective Black joy, was consciously aware we were challenging and resisting the injustices of anti-Black racism and white supremacy by occupying public space that was at the core of California's identity.

Today I take walks and I marvel at the natural and cultural landscapes that surround me. I love taking these and occasional bicycle rides along the Pacific Ocean shoreline paths, where I can feel and smell the coastal zone air. And I continue to find joy frolicking in the ocean, where I have even expanded my wave riding with surfing lessons. If my parents were alive to see me enjoying surfing, I know they would relish my traversing this public space where Black people have faced white racism and other challenges. These outdoor activities rejuvenate and inspire me in my work as a historian and a cultural producer who recovers, documents, and shares ignored stories to empower others, as I also work at being a good steward of our Earth.

Alison Rose Jefferson, MHC, PhD, is a historian, heritage conservation consultant, and third-generation Californian. Her book, *Living the California Dreams: African American Leisure Sites During the Jim Crow Era*, was honored with the 2020 Miriam Matthews Ethnic History Award by the Los Angeles City Historical Society for its exceptional contributions to the greater understanding and awareness of regional history.

Places of Purpose

Spaces for Growth and Connection

"I see it! We're almost there!" I yelled to my sister, Delane, who followed a few yards behind me. My feet picked up pace with excitement after I finally glimpsed a hint of the glassy pond just beyond the trees at the end of the trail. From there we'd launch kayaks into the water, disrupting its smooth surface with ripples.

"Good!" Delane said with excitement, and a hint of fatigue.

At sixty years old, this would be my sister's first time kayaking. We had been on a quest to enjoy some beach time in Martha's Vineyard before going back home to California that afternoon. We'd followed our hosts' detailed directions that led us across a busy country road from our cottage to a well-maintained, wide, and bucolic grassy trail that led us to the beach. It was a treat to come from the West Coast's rugged coastline, sculpted by its earthquakes, to a place on the other side of the country where it is so easy to access the beach.

As we approached a mixed rack of several kayaks, canoes, and paddle boards, I quickly untied one of the two-person kayaks, pulled it down, and with a *thud*, it fell onto the grass. I slid the kayaks down to the dock on what remained of our trail to the water's edge. We put on life jackets fished from the storage cubby. My sister grabbed our two paddles, and we headed for the dock nearby.

I jumped up on the dock's wobbly metal floor, steadying my footing, and calculated that the platform sat nearly four feet above the water, apparently at low tide. I looked back at the kayak we'd dragged to the water's edge, then back to the dock's edge, where we stood. With her delicate knees, Delane couldn't jump from a four-foot dock or lower herself down by her arms into the tippy kayak.

For a moment, I wasn't sure how we were going to make this adventure happen. In my predicament, I thought, *If I can't figure out how to get my sister into this damn kayak, I'm in the wrong profession!*

Standing there with the gentle water beneath us still and the morning sun smooth against our faces, I knew—no matter what—I was taking my sister kayaking. She belonged in nature with me.

Delane and I had arrived in Martha's Vineyard three days earlier. I was there to speak with an organization about diversity—how they might connect more Black people to the public lands they stewarded. It was my first time in Martha's Vineyard, an island off the coast of Massachusetts and ancestral home of the native Wampanoag. I had been hearing about it for most of my adult life and knew of its contemporary reputation as a destination place of leisure for the Black *bourgeoisie,* where one might spot any number of celebrities, artists, politicians, and other notables strolling about town, as inconspicuous as anyone else on island time.

The epicenter for Black people on the island is Oak Bluffs and its adjacent beach, nicknamed The Inkwell. Some say the beach's nickname mocks the presence of Black skin in the clear edges of the Atlantic ocean; others say the name was inspired by the large number of historic Black visiting professionals, intelligentsia, and artists such as Dr. Henry Louis Gates Jr., Paul Robeson, and Ethel Waters, who all found both respite and inspiration. Regardless of its namesake, The Inkwell is a source of deep pride and belonging for Black America.

Martha's Vineyard welcomed Black people starting in the eighteenth century as the site for integrated church camp revivals. Eventually, that opened the door for Black domestic and maritime workers to purchase property, creating an enclave in Oak Bluffs that established a retreat for Black working-class folks. There is a notable connection and ease between Black and white people on the island, which can be attributed to these beginnings. During my time there, I experienced a depth of welcoming and refuge.

Today, Oak Bluffs' newest generation of property owners stand on the shoulders of the Black people who created this community, some of whom passed down homes through as many as seven generations.

One thing I love most about the island is its seaside charm of patinated wood-shingled homes, with generous porches and

"These welcoming nature spaces—places of purpose—represent how Black people have persisted over decades, through blatant exclusion from public recreation and codified Jim Crow laws, to still create our own Black justice, joy, and healing in nature."

easy chairs. These homes are built to be resilient to the salty sea air, and nature's touch was evident wherever I looked and felt in the spongy spring of its dirt paths under my feet. What reigns supreme is an outdoor lifestyle, grounded by the values and needs of the people who pilgrimage there, seeking refuge from their urban lives.

We experienced this firsthand at a brunch event hosted by a female Black finance tech entrepreneur. We enjoyed delicious crab cake Benedict with authors, academics, political pundits, actors, and investors who created a down-home atmosphere and a call to action to welcome and offer refuge to anyone, no matter who they are.

Black people having a connection and a sense of place in nature is nothing new. Historic Black gathering places, like Oak Bluffs, have existed for many years. From Southern screened wraparound porches, to urban backyards, to the secret fishing spots under a bridge visited on Sunday afternoons, to even more formal places of retreat—these locations are forged and held lovingly by Black people and for Black people to gather and belong joyously in nature.

After emancipation from slavery, Black people created enclaves across the United States for outdoor retreat, such as Lincoln Hills in Colorado, Idlewild in Michigan, and camps for children and families that sprung up along the East and West Coast forests in the early twentieth century. These welcoming nature spaces—places of purpose—represent how Black people have persisted over decades, through blatant exclusion from public recreation and codified Jim Crow laws, to still create our own Black justice, joy, and healing in nature.

Living my whole life in the San Francisco Bay Area, I am no stranger to scenic beauty in nature all around. But few areas in California have the multigenerational rootedness of a Black presence in nature, such as what I have discovered in places like Oak Bluffs, and many other historic places across the country. Had it not been for my experiences at our family ranch and Oakland's Feather River Family camp, I might have missed out on the feeling of belonging in nature in California, where Black populations are still comparatively new in this part of our young nation.

Not everyone can access iconic Black havens in the outdoors, or have a family history of connecting to them, yet it is critical for everyone to have the opportunity to get away from it all, and it is why I have devoted my work to helping Black people

experience healing, peace, and resilience in the restorative elements of nature.

In this section, you'll find reflections by people who have found their own places of purpose that range from destinations and pilgrimages over generations, such as Massachusetts's historic Camp Atwater, as described by our eldest contributor, Cordelia "Betty" Hinkson Brown; or perhaps it is a tale of an unexpected discovery at sunrise along a sandstone path in a New Mexico desert, found in Antoine Skinner's "Finding Creation on a Sandstone Ridge;" or a deep meditation of what might be observed just beyond the frame of a window in Camille Dungy's poem, "A Clearing." I'm hopeful these contributions will ignite your own memories of joyful exploration, while inspiring more recognition and celebration of special places in nature,

"Not everyone can access iconic Black havens in the outdoors, or have a family history of connecting to them, yet it is critical for everyone to have the opportunity to get away from it all, and it is why I have devoted my work to helping Black people experience healing, peace, and resilience in the restorative elements of nature."

so that more generations might find their own special belonging.

The experiences my sister and I shared on Martha's Vineyard were so warm and welcoming that they helped us to connect with one another with a depth and ease we might not have had back at home amidst our own busy routines. I saw how this special place was inspiring my sister to push through her fears of outdoor exploration and try kayaking with me for the first time. I recognized that, for so many reasons, this place was a place of purpose.

Standing on that dock in Martha's Vineyard, I suddenly came up with a plan to get my sister on the water.

I could slide the kayak alongside the dock to the water's edge, and with enough of the stern in the water, my sister could ease into the cockpit much easier from that height.

I am *in the right profession*.

It was a special moment to be an aide to my older sister. To be in the right place at the right time, so that I could be a part of that first-time experience for her, just like I get to be in my work so often. Many first-time outdoor recreationists need to be in good hands in order to feel safe and welcomed.

After pushing offshore and paddling the short way to the other side of the pond, we got out and scrambled up a bluff. From the top we looked out at the vast Atlantic Ocean. Not a soul near us, we took in its beauty and peace. Then we found our way to the ocean, where we played in the waves like we were kids again—a restorative moment we needed at the end of our big trip. A moment of connection. An everlasting joy in a place of purpose.

—Rue

69

Family and Community among the Redwoods

Adimika Arthur

Along the California northern coast, there is a large community of trees that stretch hundreds of feet into the air—the coast redwoods, *Sequoia sempervirens*. Seven miles inland from the town of Mendocino, there is a camp, originally built as a recreational demonstration area by the Civilian Conservation Corps.

More than sixty years ago, a few Black women traveled to this camp and found the secret to these trees—that strength is their roots, and they built a foundation and network of powerful connections almost as tight as the redwoods' interlocking roots. They were there with their children, seeking respite from Oakland and San Francisco, but over time their connection to this place has evolved into an intergenerational celebration of community, fellowship, and heritage at Jack and Jill Family Camp.

Today, six decades after those women experienced the beauty of the coast redwoods, a unique gathering of African American family reunion-style camping continues at the shallow-root redwoods in the Mendocino Woodlands. Jack and Jill Family Camp has reframed history, braiding together the historical contributions of these mothers who pilgrimage to

the redwoods to reclaim public space and the recreation of Black people. Families—not necessarily blood-related—have stayed connected over generations and welcomed other families to the magic of the redwoods and the stability of a family camp that helps visitors unplug from the grind of work and centers the Black family unit in activities like welcoming bonfires, carnival games, and tea parties.

My family joined this ecosystem eight years ago with my father (who has since passed on to the ancestors), husband, and oldest son. Our family has since grown with the addition of another son, who first visited camp straight from the hospital delivery room. Our dedication to the tradition of a week in the redwoods is our version of "family reunion," with a chosen, created family. We descend into the redwoods for a week with fifty other families and connect in the way only nature allows you to do: with laughter from children rummaging through ferns, vibrating joy, energy, and playing ancient games of tag for hours, protected by the redwood forest floor. Midnight hikes led by teens, swimming hole activities with picnic fares, and multigenerational toes gracing the frigid waterside with R & B gracing Bluetooth speakers. Dominoes, family-style bingo, and Name that Tune are our evening activities instead of video games and work laptops.

This wisdom from nature expands communities and strengthens connections that don't involve business cards or titles. While redwoods grow where they are planted, these redwoods have planted a legacy of Black excellence, love of nature, and generational healing. Sixty years later, the redwood wilderness has become synonymous with Black liberation, family legacy, and reunion-style celebration.

Adimika Arthur is a medical tech professional, wife, and mother from Seattle. She now lives in Oakland with her family.

Boley's Black Joy

Suzette Chang

My experience of Black joy is a layered and sensory journey grounded in legacy. This is embodied in my annual trip to the Boley Rodeo and Parade. This event consists of hundreds of high-steppin' horses guided by the direction of young Black riders; dance groups (young and *seasoned*—I'll explain the word "seasoned" later), movin'-n'-shakin' their bodies with style, class, and grace to ole-skool R & B; and crowds of people, all of us with a deep sense of connection to the land called Boley, Oklahoma.

The origins of this place are full of lore. As documented in *Acres of Aspiration: The All-Black Towns in Oklahoma* by Hannibal Johnson, it is believed that this all-black town was founded as "a social experiment or a bet" (perhaps even a literal bet). As the story goes, Mr. W. H. Boley, a European American man, wagered "that Negros could prosper if given the opportunity." Whether or not the bet really took place is unknown, but this origin story has been passed down since the late 1800s; Boley became a self-sustaining town before Oklahoma statehood at the turn of the twentieth century. And, with every step taken on this land, every African American Boley resident is reminded that *we won the bet!*

This place is not without its wounds. There is a continued presence of sundown towns. The first documented lynching of an African American woman occurred at a neighboring sundown town. These difficult experiences and countless others serve as motivations for African

American people to be self-sufficient and self-aware legacy builders of this historic Oklahoma all-Black town.

As I myself step upon the land—a place of rich agriculture, tenacity, and investment—I experience deeper understanding of why my confidence is strengthened, my stride is longer, and my purpose deepened in this place. Everywhere I look, I see myself in various hues of melanated human greatness: dark chocolate, mocha, cinnamon, hazelnut, molasses, and creamy chocolate, just to name a few. To witness this is a dream come true.

As I walk through the rodeo, genuine laughter from adults and children dances around my head and within my soul because they, like me, know laughter is a necessity of life and heals many wounds. To my left is a fierce game of Bid Whist (pronounced *Bit-Wiz*, it's a four-player card game played with two teams), and loud talking; to my right are children playing jump rope or tag while wearing the full rodeo garb of boots, jeans, cowboy and cowgirl hats, and button-down shirts. I am surrounded by joy.

Touching the worn and tender hands of Boley's seasoned adults (a kinder and respectful way to say seniors or old folks) brings me deeper into my experience of Black joy. Every wrinkle and gray hair speaks to stories of fortitude, longevity, and family. As I look into their eyes, I see what is and what was built, endured, and maintained. I sit at their feet and take deep, long, and methodical breaths, filling my lungs with the knowledge that I am surrounded and am living Black joy.

As the laughter continues and smooth ole' school music is playing, my nose is tantalized with savory smells of barbecued meats seasoned and smoked to perfection with aged spices preserved by generations of the past and given to next generations with care, reverence, and humility; the sweetness of candied yams enriched with grace; savory potato salads layered with compassion and sincerity; corn on the cob kissed with butter gliding from one kernel to the next; and collard, mustard, and turnip greens, picked from local Boley gardens and cooked to perfection. I am in the presence of Black joy as I am standing upon land owned and sustained by Black people with a commitment to nurture and care for self and others. This is Black joy!

Suzette Chang is an applied-methods cultural anthropologist, lover of nature, and librarian. She is the founder and CEO of Thick Descriptions, an organization that provides educational resources to help communities better understand themselves, and the executive director of the Guthrie Public Library. She lives in Oklahoma.

Finding Creation on a Sandstone Ridge

Antoine Skinner

When I was eighteen and in the Boy Scouts, I took a group of young scouts backpacking through Cimarron, New Mexico. I was the only African American on the trip, and it was the first time I had ever done backcountry backpacking.

I recall a day during the trip when we were deep into the backcountry, upon a ridge. We had hiked about twenty-five miles that day before we set up camp. I felt like I wanted to be alone, so I got up early the next morning, hiked up to the very peak of the ridge above our camp, and sat on the sandstone. I could see the colors of the sky drip from reds to oranges to magenta into purple, and I could see those colors fade into the darkness of the alpine forest. It was the most beautiful view I had ever seen in my life.

The morning dew and mist were in the air, and while I was sitting there watching the sunrise on this sandstone ridge, taking it all in, two red-tailed hawks flew right in front of me, colliding and spinning around each other in a match. Their tails twisted and danced in the blowing wind. As I watched them fly past me, I knew, in that moment, that this was for me. I knew that I would forever love being in nature. I sat there for the rest of the early morning, watching the sun come up.

Sitting on that ridge, I thought, *Wow, how can people not believe there is a God?* I knew at that moment there was something bigger and more powerful than us that had created what I had witnessed. And I also knew I would continue to seek moments like this.

For the rest of that day, I reflected on that majestic moment. A couple of guys eventually approached me, and someone snapped a picture of me peacefully sitting there. Whenever I look at the picture, I can see the peace and contemplation on my face, the connection that I was making at that moment with nature. And for me that was it. From then I was hooked on nature for the rest of my life.

Antoine Skinner is an Outdoor Afro trip leader. He lives with his wife in Arizona.

Going Home to Nature

Evita Robinson

When I need nature, I go home.

Nature is my equilibrium. I've spent the vast majority of my adulthood living in or around New York City, and I think people automatically assume I grew up here. But I grew up in Poughkeepsie, a riverfront town a few hours north of the city. The last train stop on the Hudson Line.

The Hudson River was always the indicator I was home. Growing up, I watched the riverfront go from forgotten and decrepit, to either gentrified or rejuvenated, depending on who you asked. When I was young, the riverfront was a place of congregation for us. The parties thrown in the Pavilion, people watching on boats and jet skis, the ferry rides up to the Roundout, and summertime BBQ set ups. Sometimes you'd just go for the peace and reflection. My journals saw many pages inked on riverfront benches. Hours of writing gave way to hours of walking.

Now the old abandoned aerial train tracks connecting Poughkeepsie to Highland is a walkway in the sky. The riverfront reflected a lot of our childhoods. Our adolescence was colorful, just like the Mid-Hudson Bridge. To this day, it's my favorite bridge, with its vibrantly hued lights that go from dancing color with no rhyme or reason to asserting the city's support for the PRIDE community. I love that bridge. I love that riverfront.

Evita Turquoise Robinson is the creator of the NOMADNESS Travel Tribe community and their annual AUDACITY Fest for travelers of color and their allies. She is the recipient of AFAR's Travel Vanguard Award and was honored as one of *National Geographic's* 2021 Most Visionary Women in Travel History and *Entrepreneur* magazine's 50 Most Daring Entrepreneurs of 2018.

Blacksurfing

Rick Blocker

Surfing is simply the act of catching and riding a wave, but being a surfer means so very, very much more. Surfing is about relationships—my relationship to life, to the ocean, to the waves, to other people, and to the Earth. It's a natural activity that I bring my mind, body, and spirit to.

At first I didn't realize what I had gotten myself into, but I quickly found a new sense of adventure, excitement, and joy. Although I did not catch or ride a single wave my first day on a surfboard, I found a feeling of peace and freedom just sitting alone on my board in the water outside of the breakers. I noticed how majestically the mountains rolled down to the sand at the ocean's edge. How the orange sun hung above the western horizon. I felt the warm summer breeze lightly brush across my face. What a view! What a feeling! I floated with the tide and breathed in the clean, salty ocean air. I found home that day.

It wasn't long before I was back there having the time of my life, flying across wave after wave as free as a bird with my newfound friends at the beach. Although my parents didn't understand my new obsession for riding waves, they supported me in living my dream. They told me if I could be a surfer, I could do anything.

Being a Black surfer here in America has always been especially challenging, because many people say that Black people don't belong in the ocean. This

is simply not true. Throughout my life I have surfed with people of color all around the world. I've learned that we are the original surfers and we belong everywhere that we want to be.

I have now been surfing for more than fifty years and my passion for it and my love for nature and life have only grown. Surfing has taught me the importance of living in the now and being present. As a surfer I am a visual artist, dancer, and acrobat with a unique way of approaching life. I study the changing tides, swell angles, cloud formations, and wind conditions to inform me how best to live life. Because of my relationship with the ocean's energy and nature's rhythm, I am able to face challenges head-on while recognizing my limitations. To hug the pocket when it opens up and glide through the smoother sections with style and grace. Life is riding a wave.

The new generation of young surfers of color are boldly reclaiming our place in the lineup. I am so proud of them for creating a new aquatic community founded in social justice, freedom, equality, and Black pride. They show the world that in the water, Black Lives Matter too.

Today I have a smile. I've lived a good life. I'm grateful for having been blessed to be a lifelong advocate for diversity and inclusion in the surf community. I have traveled to some of the most incredible surf spots, ridden waves with dolphins and seals, and met some of the most amazing people. People who are honest and humble enough to call themselves simply surfers. That is who I am. A Black surfer. May you, too, find your joy.

Rick Blocker is a retired teacher and lifelong surfer based in Los Angeles. He has been an advocate for diversity and inclusion in surfing for more than fifty years. Rick is an original member of the Black Surfing Association and his surfing exploits were featured in the 2011 documentary *White Wash*, a film about African American surf culture.

A Clearing

Camille Dungy

all night the wind blows   & my mind
          my mind is like the crabapple that loses
limbs   they litter the ground   crush
          the black-eyed susan   scatter buds
over rows of new lettuce   bean sprouts
          whose fresh greens are clusters of worry
in raised beds   blown leaves & cracked limbs
          threaten the foundation   water backs up
in gutters seeps into the house's walls

but my mind is not in the house

in the yard's far corner the eye of my mind rests
          on the crabapple   shaken   snapping
hectic   then still   the day dawns
          without anger   the blue jay I've looked for
pushes sky off his crest   how splendid
          his wings & tail   it's not so much
that before this he'd hidden himself
          it's only he favored a branch
I could not see until the storm thinned the tree

Camille Dungy is a poet, author, and professor. Her honors include a 2019 Guggenheim Fellowship, an American Book Award, two NAACP Image Award Nominations, and fellowships from the National Endowment for the Arts in both prose and poetry. She currently resides with her husband and daughter in Colorado.

Outside Is Calling My Name

Tiara Phalon

Lately my relationship to the outside has meant traveling the world and considering myself a global citizen. Traveling begs the question, *Who am I in relation to other cultures?* And it leads to tough conversations about how we as Black Americans should be conscious of our footprint in places where people are less fortunate than we are, people who are not able to get on a plane for a vacation, or adventure outside in the ways we have.

Over the last couple of years my wanderlust has taken me to the Dominican Republic, Mexico, and Rwanda, to name a few. I had the opportunity to play with language, eat amazing foods, and consider that maybe I was "American first" and "Black second" overseas—a perspective I didn't enjoy but experienced along the way. That bit of culture shock did not erase the immense amount of joy I felt to just get away.

Outside in Punta Cana, Dominican Republic, I embarked upon four-wheeler excursions through the countryside, as I clutched my pearls from the passenger seat and tasted the clay of red mud that splashed in my face. I remembered that I was alive, and that this is one of many things outside has to offer. I watched children run through the countryside, barefoot, offering flowers in return for a dollar. I remember wishing I had more and promising myself that I would be better prepared next time to make a contribution because their island reminded me that sometimes I actually am free.

Outside in Mexico I found myself topless on a beach in Tulum. It was wild and liberating.

I was surrounded by Black women I loved and trusted. I stood and gazed at the ocean like an urban mermaid sunbathing near the shore. My spirit said a silent prayer: "Dear God, more of this." I sat at the feet of the pyramids at Chichen Itza, and looked up in wonder at the culturally infused designs of those who aligned holy things with the sun, moon, and stars—recognizing a people who understood the importance of nature, recognizing that my ancestors created wonders like this and that maybe this trip was an invitation back to my ancient self.

Outside in Rwanda, my whole family spent days on a lazy lake called Muhazi. We fell off the sides of canoes and kayaks during the day, and listened to the hum of crickets and songs of bats at night. It was the serenity of the earth and the outdoors wrapping itself around us, protecting us, offering us a moment of calm in a world that felt like it had lost its everlasting mind! We practiced archery, zip-lined, and rode horses at a ranch called Fazenda Sengha.

All of these adventures helped me see myself as a daughter of the world. As someone whose presence means something. I never considered myself outdoorsy, but I look at it all differently now. Perhaps I won't hike Mount Kilimanjaro, but you can for sure find me outside, on somebody's beach, sweaty, and welcoming the breezes from around the world on my sticky skin. I'll always welcome the opportunity to bond in nature and do something new, fun, and scary. To find a reprieve and holistic therapy being in nature's elements.

Outside owes me nothing.

But I owe it my gratitude.

Tiara Phalon is a world traveler and educator living in California with her husband and three children.

Camp Atwater

Cordelia "Betty" Hinkson Brown

In the spring of 1933, when I was ten, my family returned to our home in Philadelphia after living in Europe, where my father, Dr. DeHaven Hinkson, completed his advanced studies in obstetrics and gynecology. My mother, her sister, and their friends were keen on the idea of attending the World's Fair in Chicago that summer. Fortunately for us, they discovered Camp Atwater, a summer camp for Black children in Massachusetts established by the Urban League in 1921, and decided that the camp was the ideal place to leave me, my sister, Mary, and my cousins while they took their trip to the fair. Their discovery was the beginning of a rich and wonderful adventure that left us with splendid memories for life.

Our time at Camp Atwater introduced us to enjoyable outdoor activities that we would cherish for the rest of our lives, and expanded our circle of friends and our social network extensively. The campers, boys in the month of July and the girls for the month of August, traveled to North Brookfield, Massachusetts, via multiple train cars from up and down the East Coast, including Boston, New Haven, New York, Philadelphia, Washington, D.C., Baltimore, and Richmond. Together, we formed a very cohesive and close-knit community of African American (then referred to as "Colored" or "Negro") youths.

The camp was situated on beautiful Lake Lashaway, which provided a perfect setting for programs centered around aquatic sports. Our camp

time was dominated by physical education and challenges designed to advance our swimming proficiency. The youngest campers learned to swim in shallow waters of the lake, and each year we were taught and encouraged to swim farther and farther out until we were able to reach an island in the lake. The reward for swimming to the island was to be able to move into a cabin, or "hut," as we called them, for the season. Archery, marksmanship, all sorts of games, music, and talent shows were among the many other camp activities, but swimming and the lake were the center of everything.

Those summers we spent on Lake Lashaway with our friends, new and old, were extraordinarily special. They gave us a great sense of freedom, independence, and confidence in ourselves. Above all, we had great fun and made good friends. At ninety-eight, I still look back with joy at the time I spent at camp! I know and appreciate how fortunate we were to have had those years at Camp Atwater.

After camp Atwater, Cordelia "Betty" Hinkson Brown went on to graduate from Cornell University and attend graduate school at the Universidad Nacional Autónoma de México and the University of Wisconsin. Now ninety-nine, Betty lives in Detroit, Michigan where she raised her family, taught Head Start and third grade, and remains a community activist. These days, her outdoor pleasure comes from her lovely garden and watching the neighborhood children play.

A Cabin Wall in Lincoln Hills

Shonda Scott

There is so much history held in our family's cabin in Lincoln Hills, in the Rocky Mountains of Colorado. This history goes back to my great grandfather, who was a son of an enslaved Black woman and a white slave owner. He was born enslaved, but after he was emancipated, he became a developer in Lincoln Hills—a segregated area outside of Denver where Black families could build their own resort cabins. In the 1920s, my great grandfather moved his family—my grandmother and her sister—from Missouri to Colorado and built the cabin in 1926. It remains in our family to this day.

Visits to the cabin have become a part of our family's tradition for almost one hundred years. My aunt, who is now the family matriarch, is ninety-six years old and has been visiting the cabin since she was two years old. Now, five generations later, my son, my cousins, and all their kids go to that cabin that still stands.

The cabin became a destination for special family moments, and for retreat. My parents had their honeymoon in the family cabin. My cousin, who just retired from being a judge in Denver, went to the cabin to study for the bar as a law student.

The cabin is also a destination for family gatherings. Everybody meets up at the cabin and we hike to the top of the mountain. There is always a fun pecking order to determine who gets to go or do something first, like the cabin tasks, or other outdoor adventures. My father hiked to the top of the mountain when he was eighty years old, making him the reigning champion as the oldest member of the family to do so.

My son has been going to the cabin with my dad since he was seventeen months old. It's their annual trip and they always stay at the cabin. My son took interest in a visiting squirrel he named Nutty, and Nutty was always there. Of course Nutty was likely a new squirrel each year, visiting my son, scrambling among the pine trees year after year.

Our cabin has also become a museum that celebrates the history of my family, Black excellence, and the notable people who touched all our lives.

Eventually, my brother and I created a documentary to record our family history centered around the cabin—we found that everybody had a story to tell about their moments at the cabin, and in the process, I learned some new things about what the cabin has meant to different members of our family.

My cousin, the oldest girl in the family, is our family historian. Our family history is showcased on a cabin wall and it honors and celebrates notable people our family has met, their honors and distinctions. I have pictures of President Obama and I, when I served on his presidential platform committee, and photos from when delegates of the Democratic National Convention from across the country visited our cabin in 2008. There is a photo of my cousin and I when we each met President Clinton, and more historical figures that our family members met over the years. We also have the photos of my dad and uncles, who served in the military during war times, with their commendation letters and the awards they achieved during their service.

And of course there is the photo of my great grandfather, who built the cabin, and my great grandmother.

As our family's young people visit and see these images and artifacts, they can experience a special connection to our family history—we've known and have been able to trace our history back to slavery, even before they had Ancestry.com!

In 2020, our cabin was designated by Gilpin County as a historic building, joining other notable Lincoln Hills landmarks, including the historic Wink's Lodge. Wink's Lodge was a hotel that hosted great talents like Ella Fitzgerald and Lena Horne, performers who couldn't stay in Denver because of segregation.

There is so much Black history and my own family history in Lincoln Hills. I treasure sharing these stories with others, and treasure knowing that the history will be passed on to my son and generations to come.

Shonda Scott is an award-winning CEO, distinguished business leader, and fourth-generation entrepreneur. Shonda's passions are TV production, travel, writing, and international affairs. Born in Oakland, California, her family roots in Denver, Colorado, go back to the 1920s.

A Birthday with Wild Dolphins

Elaine Lee

I am a Cancer. It's my zodiac sign, and one of the four astrological signs governed by the planetary element of water. And for this water baby, water is my home away from home!

I have loved water sports as long as I can remember, starting with swimming lessons at age five at Idlewild Lake, a Black resort in northern Michigan, where my family spent the better part of every summer. There I learned not only to swim, but also to fish, motorboat, and water ski. After graduating from college, I moved to California, where my water adventures expanded to include sailing, surfing, whitewater rafting, houseboating, and becoming a long-distance fitness swimmer.

The one water adventure I longed for, but had never experienced, was to swim with wild dolphins. A "dolphin quest" adventure seemed like it would be a wonderful birthday present to give to myself, as well as a perfect hiatus from the rigors of work, family dramas, and my ever-elusive love life.

To put the wheels in motion I called my friend Paul, who had a beach house on the Kona coast of the Big Island of Hawaii, and asked him if I could visit for a week or so. He enthusiastically welcomed me. The trip was on!

The night before my birthday I started getting excited for our dolphin swim. I prepared our lunch, got my snorkeling gear together, and set my watch alarm for 6:50 a.m. That would give me enough time to pick up the kayak and drive twenty minutes to Kealakekua Bay to greet the dolphins at their alleged bewitching hour of 8:00 a.m., the time they usually would come from the ocean into the bay.

But Paul's plans unexpectedly changed, and even though he tried his best to find someone else to go with me, I decided I would go it alone.

After pulling up to the pier at 1:30 p.m., later than planned, I looked out into the ocean and, to my surprise, I saw dozens of spinner dolphins playing in the bay. I knew I would have to join them, but they were so far out—maybe a mile or two—*Could I do it?* I wondered. *Of course,* I thought. *I am a long-distance fitness swimmer!*

But as I walked back to the car to retrieve my goggles and fins, fear began to nibble away at my courage as I pondered the distance of the journey and the size of the ocean waves. I felt very small and alone. So I summoned up my Warrior Woman spirit to mentally prepare myself for the aquatic adventure. As I headed across the parking lot, I spotted a woman and her dog driving up in a truck. She quickly jumped out and started putting on a wetsuit. I hollered out, "Are you going to swim with the dolphins?" She nodded yes and I said, "Can I go with you?" and she said "Yes, but I am in a hurry, so you will have to keep up!"

"Hallelujah," I said to myself as I scurried behind her. She mentioned that she lived down the street and had gotten word that the dolphins were running late today, so she decided to get in a visit with them before her next appointment.

She ran to the beach, donned her snorkeling gear, and jumped in, and I followed right behind her. The waves were quite active that day, so it was hard for me to see her at times, but there were four kayaks circling the current dolphin gathering area, so I focused on them. Despite my fierce efforts to gauge my route, the powerful waves continually pushed me off my intended course. At long last, thirty to forty minutes later, I arrived at a playground of dozens of gray, silver, and white spinner dolphins. A constellation of emotions greeted me: excitement, relief, fear, joy, and astonishment. I found myself feeling overwhelmed as I looked back at the distant shoreline and gazed down to the ocean floor below, some eighty feet away.

As I worked to overcome my fears, the woman from the parking lot swam over to me and welcomed me to the bay of dolphins. She expressed her surprise at my ability to keep up with her. She proceeded to give me a mini lesson in dolphinese, such as how to make the dolphin noises and mimic their swimming style to make them feel more comfortable around us and increase the probability of true interaction.

Sunbeams pierced the water's surface, sending cylindrical streams of light to the ocean floor. The dolphins whirled, glided, spun, and splashed through the streams in a kaleidoscopic dance of water, light, and motion that seemed choreographed by the gods, yet totally spontaneous. It was a spectacular natural high to witness these glorious creatures in their natural habitat just being their regular dolphin selves—creating so much beauty, while being joyous and free. Pumping their tails to accelerate speed, they would often spin themselves into the air and nosedive back down to pierce the ocean's surface. I found their size, speed, and large numbers initially alarming but remarkably fascinating.

We hung out with the dolphins for about an hour and then the woman reminded me that she had an appointment and that it was time for her to leave. As we departed, a pod of six or so dolphins ushered us back to shore. They swam about three feet directly under us as we mimicked one another's moves and sounds. What a touching goodbye from my newfound marine family.

When we got back to the parking lot, I thanked the woman for her presence and guidance. Still awash in wonder from our new connection and shared experience, we bid each other farewell.

My afternoon at Kealakekua Bay was a precious and perfect birthday gift from the sea—a holy communion of serendipity and fortitude that brought a stillness to my soul, a lightness to my spirit, and joy to my heart.

Elaine Lee is a travel journalist and the editor of *Go Girl: The Black Woman's Book of Travel and Adventure*. She has taken two solo trips around the world and has visited sixty-five countries. To learn more about Elaine, visit www.ugogurl.com.

Hands on
the Land

Sustenance and Connection

A favorite staple in our family meals were collard greens. We would grow them in our garden on the ranch using compost and leveraging the sunny climate of Lake County to produce the biggest, sturdiest green leaves you ever did see or taste. Always bountiful, our garden produced rows and rows of vegetables nearly year-round. Whatever we did not eat, we packed up to enjoy back home in Oakland, or preserved for later.

Harvesting food and animals was a way of life in our family, and an important part of how we experienced the natural world. There was something for everyone on this land, and every part of nature was met with respect.

A variety of fruit trees and grapevines grew on the property, from which we made wine—something sweet the adults could sip in the sunshine. Most of the fruits ripened heaviest in the fall and summer: pears, plums, peaches, and apples, perfect for picking a snack after a swim. When we had a surplus, we'd have a canning party among the women, making jams and preserves while gossiping together around the table. We enjoyed the sweet tastes of those fruits all year long.

A barn stood beyond the house and inside we stored my dad's big, olive-green motorboat that we used for fishing expeditions. Perched on a trailer, the boat looked so big, but once in the water, its heavy bottom would all but disappear.

My first memory of fishing is from around the age of four. The excitement of a tight line released a squeal of excitement from me. As the flopping fish, its mouth opened so big and wide, was reeled to the surface and netted into the boat, I exclaimed, "Daddy, Daddy, the fish is *laughing!*" At home in the kitchen, my mom scaled, gutted, and cut up the fish to be seasoned and rolled in cornmeal for a fish fry. Whatever was left over was stored in old

plastic or paper milk cartons, in water, and frozen to eat, for another time or to share with others.

When we weren't out on the water fishing, we were tending the land of the ranch, where our red barn stood, filled with hay and feed for our livestock. At one point we had one horse, two cows, and a heavy, tired sow who eventually sired nine pigs that would become pork. Almost every part of the pig was processed by our family for eating. Many parts were for delicacies that are now considered rare, such as chitterlings, the large intestine; hog "maws," the stomach; and "hog head cheese," an amalgam of the meat from the snout and other flesh from a pig's head, which would

"These experiences also helped me appreciate the importance of a community in nature—and in the case of traditional soul food, it typically requires a lot of helping hands to bring that good food to the dinner table to feed the mind, body, and spirit across generations, and it helps us to remember who we are."

be made into a vinegary terrine. Those foods, once considered useless scraps and a symbol of Black suffering, are also a reminder of the ingenuity and creativity of a people who knew how to make a way out of no way.

Some of the foods we enjoyed on the ranch are now frowned upon or stigmatized. I recently asked some Black friends how many times per week they ate soul food. The answers were surprising. Many rushed in with "Never!" or the reluctant "Only on special occasions," and "I gave it up years ago."

These responses revealed to me that the foods of our heritage are too often seen as part of a stigma to be overcome and distanced from. This narrative represented such a different world view from the one that I was raised with and the experiences I had with foods that had been sustainably captured, processed, and shared with so much joy on our family's ranch.

My privilege, having had these experiences as an urban girl, came into sharper focus, along with the essence of what soul food is really about. Soul food simmers in deep pots and large cast-iron pans—food meant for the community by design. Soul food is also *very* American. From the menu at a Boston Market to New American bistros, and oxtail dishes served out of food trucks, these were all the same foods my ancestors made with painstaking perfection and locally sourced for their own families, for households as enslaved people, or as hired cooks in inns, hotel restaurants, and dining trains. Food made from those hands had the power to strengthen and sustain the hearts and souls of my ancestors, and it has endured, worthy of honoring and preserving for lifetimes to come.

Today, I am a hunter and harvester, and strive to make most of my meals from scratch, using seasonal ingredients from my local farmer's market. I try to avoid fast food, which is an easy temptation for busy, working families and commuters like me and my own. I've been pleased to discover ways to weave these connections to the land into my daily life. For instance, there are beautiful, abundant cherry trees in my backyard. From those trees, I love making cherry jam and sharing these jams with friends and others as an expression of love and community. Just as I learned on that ranch as a child.

The ability of Black people to find sustenance through our connection to land is a timeless way of being. My early lessons on the ranch in harvesting fruits, vegetables, and wild and domesticated animals has made me value knowing where my food comes from. These experiences also helped me appreciate the importance of a community in nature—and in the case of traditional soul food, it typically requires a lot of helping hands to bring that good food to the dinner table to feed the mind, body, and spirit across generations, and it helps us to remember who we are. I feel like my ancestors smile every time I take a bite of these heritage foods.

For the enslaved Black people of the South, hunting, fishing, and trapping skills meant the ability to supplement poor provisions, and it was a source of pride to be able to nourish one's family. These connections remain with us. Representing a modern wave of intention and purpose, the contributors in this section paint beautiful portraits that show how they are continuing to draw from nature's abundant bounty. In the upcoming pages you will find Jonathan Wilkins share his passion for hunting for his Arkansas family in "Sustenance"; learn about Detroit Hives, an urban beekeeping initiative that imparts the lessons we can learn from honey bees; and read about Tamu Curtis, a drink mixologist from Charlotte, North Carolina, who explains why natural elements in cocktails will leave you feeling better with every sip.

—Rue

Catching Joy

Angelo Paez

Nature and the outdoors first truly sparked my interest while attending my first year at California State University, Monterey Bay. I made good friends with my baseball teammate Hunter, and we took small fishing trips all over Monterey, Carmel, and Seaside, enjoying a variety of fishing methods due to the abundance of freshwater and saltwater fish life—pier fishing, shore fishing, poke pulling between the rocks, kayak fishing, and boat fishing.

One day we decided to try a new location at the end of the Salinas River we didn't know existed. Upon arrival we noticed that the parking location was for public hunting grounds, full of empty shotgun shells. We carefully hiked through the grounds until we got to the beach, where we progressed for two more miles. The location we arrived at was something I had never dealt with before: the Salinas River had connected to the bay and created a brackish marine environment in which fish had been naturally trapped by the fluctuating tides. A cove was formed at the end with sand while the rocky banks of the river developed the perfect fishing spot.

We set up our poles with lures and were ready to cast. As soon as the lures hit the water we immediately hooked up with fish. After putting up a fierce fight, we were finally able to get our fish in to see what we caught. My first-ever beautiful striped bass weighed in at fifteen pounds!

With adrenaline coursing through my body, I felt invincible. Although the joy and excitement of catching this fish was amazing, it took the journey to

finally receive this gift that made this experience worth it. From this moment forward I have been drawn to outdoor activities more than ever and have been able to explore more of my outdoor interests, such as gardening and hunting. The serenity and tranquility of being outdoors gives me time to reflect and appreciate my journey of experiences throughout life.

Angelo Paez is a student at San Jose State, majoring in biological science. He loves fishing, hunting, and gardening and hopes to one day look back proudly at all his adventures in nature, in spite of insecurities or stereotypes about who can enjoy the outdoors.

Healing through Farming

Leah Penniman

As a young Black child raised in the rural northeast, it was very difficult for me to understand who I was and where I belonged. Some of the children in our conservative, almost all-white, public school taunted, bullied, and assaulted me and my siblings, and I was confused and horrified by their malice. But while the school was often terrifying, I found solace in the forest. When humans were too much to bear, the earth consistently held firm under my feet and the solid, sticky trunk of the majestic white pine offered me something stable to grasp. I imagined that I was alone in identifying with Earth as Sacred Mother, having no idea that my African ancestors were transmitting their cosmology to me, whispering across time, "Hold on, daughter—we won't let you fall."

I never dreamed that I would become a farmer. As my race consciousness evolved in my teenage years, I got the message loud and clear that Black activists were concerned with gun violence, housing discrimination, and education reform, while white folks were concerned with organic farming and environmental conservation. I felt that I had to choose between "my people" and the Earth, that my dual loyalties were pulling me apart and negating my inherent right to belong. Fortunately, my ancestors had other plans. I passed by a flyer advertising a summer farming job in Boston that promised applicants the opportunity to grow food and serve the urban community. I was blessed to be accepted into the program, and from the first day, when the scent of freshly harvested cilantro nestled into my finger creases and dirty sweat stung my eyes, I was hooked on farming. Something profound and magical happened to me as I learned to plant, tend, and harvest, and later to prepare and serve that produce in Boston's toughest neighborhoods. I found an anchor in the elegant simplicity of working the Earth and sharing her bounty. What I was doing was good, right, and uncomplicated. Shoulder-to-shoulder with my peers of all hues, feet planted firmly in the earth, stewarding life-giving crops for the community—I was home. And I was a farmer.

I continued to study on farms across the northeastern United States and internationally in Ghana, Mexico, Haiti, and Vieques. While working in Ghana, my teachers, the elder Queen Mothers of Odumase Krobo, admonished me in disbelief: "Is it true that in the United States, a farmer will put the seed into the ground and not pour any libations, offer any prayers, sing, or dance, and expect that seed to grow?" Met with my ashamed silence, they continued, "That is why you are all sick! Because you see the Earth as a thing and not a being." This powerful interaction reminded me that ecological humility is part of the cultural heritage of Black people. While our 400-plus-year immersion in racial capitalism has attempted to squash that connection to the sacred Earth, there are those who persist in believing that the land and waters are family members, and who cling to our ancestral ways of knowing.

This reverence for nature infuses my life work at Soul Fire Farm, an Afro-Indigenous community farm dedicated to uprooting racism and seeding sovereignty in the food system. Our work includes farmer training for Black

and Brown growers, reparations and land return initiatives for northeast farmers, food justice workshops for urban youth, home gardens for city-dwellers whose diets suffer because of inherent racism, doorstep harvest delivery for food-insecure households, and systems and policy education for public decision-makers. We are reclaiming our rightful place of belonging on land and carrying on the legacy of our ancestors, who braided seeds in their hair before being forced onto slave ships.

We are now acutely aware of the fractures in our system of runaway consumption and corporate insatiability. We feel the hot winds of wildfire, the disruptions of pandemic, and the choked breath of the victims of state violence. We know there is no going back to "normal." The path forward demands that we take our rightful places as the younger siblings in creation, deferring to the oceans, forests, and mountains as our teachers.

Those whose skin is the color of soil are reviving their ancestral and ancient practice of listening to the earth to know which way to go. As the scientist and botanist Dr. George Washington Carver said, "How do I talk to a little flower? Through it I talk to the Infinite. And what is the Infinite? It is that silent, small force. . . that still small voice."

Leah Penniman (li/she/ya/elle) is a Black Kreyol farmer/peyizan, mother, soil nerd, author, and food justice activist from Soul Fire Farm in Grafton, New York. She cofounded Soul Fire Farm in 2010 with the mission to end racism in the food system and reclaim an ancestral connection to land.

Every Blade of Grass

Dudley Edmondson

Trying to get Black folks to understand their ownership of public lands is central to everything that I do. It's my life's work, really.

I hope to inspire people with my photographic work and some of the things I've written. With my book, *Black and Brown Faces in America's Wild Places*, I tried to create a set of outdoor role models for the African American community by simply showing them people and stories they can relate to, and in turn, it may get people to understand that the outdoors belongs to everybody.

If you're standing on a mountaintop with millions of acres of public lands laid out below you, then for all practical purposes at that moment every tree, blade of grass, and body of water on that land belongs to you—after all, you're the taxpaying public and that's who public land belongs to. That's very powerful knowledge.

Nature has a way of stripping things down to the essential and the basic. It allows me to get away from the manmade (unnatural) world and escape my human form and ways of thinking. I try to see everything for what it really is and become nothing but observation and thought in my attempts to understand it all. That is one of the many gifts of nature exposure.

You can lay down your burden in the wilderness, and take advantage of its restorative powers; I'm not sure enough African Americans know that. In wild places you can be yourself without all the pressures of society. Nobody judges you, expects you to think or act a certain way. For African Americans, this can be extremely liberating and healing—it gives you time to consider who you really are, to understand yourself in ways you never could in an urban space. To me that's freedom, medicine, and I wish I could help every Black person in America experience it.

Dudley Edmondson is an author, photographer, birder, and champion of helping more people connect to nature. He lives with his wife Nancy in Minnesota.

Reflecting in Green

The Nelson Sisters, Taylor and Teralynn

Before the soles of my feet meet the wooden floor as I wake, I am eager
to see what new melody the day bears

The dewy breeze dances to a poised beat

I inhale and it fills my soul with delight

As I close my eyes, I find myself in a pasture of green bliss

A humble abode away from countless hours of wasted days

Carrot painted poppies play hide and seek, but I always emerge in
triumph—I must—for the beauty of the perennial plant is something that
should not be taken for granted

The beauty of God's bountiful earth is unappreciated, unalleviated from
man's tamperings

Yet I stand here admiring the prancing deer and listening to the birds

harmonize, creating a tune so sweet

As busy bees bring forth new life amongst the daffodils and lilies

I lose myself to the motion of the tides

Pushing and pulling alike as my thoughts sway

Existing in the midst of this carefully crafted ecosystem, I am enchanted by its properties

I feel them flow from the tips of my hair follicles to the tips of my fingers

Inhale the sun, and go forth in greatness

I alleviate my body from all stress and find myself anew

Refreshing myself on the simplest humanities as I feel the tall blades of grass amongst the thick reeds invade my sensations, surrounding my spirit with enticing forbearance before I embark on a ceaseless migration of tribulation

Concluding this spiritual journey I am now an eternal butterfly

Taylor and Teralynn Nelson are sisters from Oakland, California. They are award-winning orators, and active leaders in their family's church.

A Toast to Nature

Tamu Curtis

I am a professional mixologist, and my passion for making cocktails began with my connection to the natural world.

I've always thrived in nature: the greenery, trees, the great outdoors. My family loved tent camping and I grew up in a house with a front yard, a backyard with grass, and a little garden. Since my childhood, I've always had a desire to have nature around my home. It gives me peace of mind.

When I moved to Los Angeles for college and stayed as a young adult, I made sure to live in apartments that had a front yard with grass and a backyard. But after many years, I decided to move downtown into an apartment on the twentieth floor of a high-rise. I had been lured to the downtown because this was the *happening* spot, where everyone was moving to be close to restaurants and entertainment, but for me, moving there felt like it went against who I truly was, and all the nature I had was contained in a little apartment balcony. I quickly found it soul crushing. I was unhappy, unmotivated.

My parents lived in Charlotte, and whenever I visited them, I marveled at how pretty their landscape was. So green. I loved it. The more I visited them, the more I found myself drawn to the area because I loved the openness of it.

Eventually I moved there. Now I have all the grass and trees that I want in my backyard—and I have my piece of mind. Even when things may not go my way, I don't have that dark cloud over me because I can go outside and see the big blue sky or clouds. Nature is all around me.

I'm growing mint, basil, and rosemary in my yard. Everything grows so abundant out here. It's true farm-to-table! I really didn't realize what that meant until I moved to North Carolina. You buy fresh food from farms that are within two miles. You know the farmers who grow your food.

Being in these beautiful, natural surroundings that speak to my soul has allowed me to grow professionally. After moving to Charlotte, I started The Cocktailery, a beverage company that sells spirits and teaches people about the art of making cocktails. I love teaching people how to make better cocktails simply by using elements of nature. Things you can grow at home. When people think of alcohol or they think of cocktails, they often think of getting trashed or drinking too much. But cocktails don't have to be unhealthy. When I make cocktails, I use fresh ingredients—it's better overall. I believe in using freshly squeezed juices from citrus and fresh herbs from my garden to counteract the *spirit*, or the ethanol. Sometimes I'll use some natural sugars, or some honey. Using agave in a cocktail won't make you feel like crap the next day!

When you make drinks with natural ingredients, you can create a multilay-ered, multidimensional cocktail that has multiple flavor profiles going on. My cocktails will make you smile.

I like seeing people interact with cocktails in an uplifting way—I want to change their perspective. I educate people about the ingredients to use, and why the body can process natural ingredients better than drinking something like a premade margarita mix that, by the end of the day, gives you a pounding headache!

I want people to drink better by adding nature into the mix. Nature is the body's healer. Let's toast to that!

Tamu Curtis is the founder of The Cocktailery, a company that makes the process of crafting cocktails more approachable for at-home drink enthusiasts. She takes pride in being able to change people's perception of what bar industry professionals look like. She lives in Charlotte, North Carolina.

Sustenance

Jonathan Wilkins

I sustain myself, find my own way, feel my own feelings. I do this with the Delta sun beating down on me while my khaki-colored skin becomes browner. Or, in the winter, when the cold turns my hands to craggy, aching things, I do this with a shotgun or a hook and line. Simple methods where technique matters. I breathe life into forgotten places and have breath blown back into me. The hot, humid breath of the American South. Air that hangs like a laundry line full of wet blankets. Omnipresent. Comforting.

I navigate bayous by boat and clumsy, muddy footsteps. Slips of navigable water between the cypress and the tupelo trees. Gnarled roots and insects abound. The birds are iridescent and the light dappled. I fish and hunt. I feed my family. I exist. Without the expectations of others. Without limits. A part of the arboraceous, skeletal structures that dominate that landscape. It's not solace I'm looking for in these wild places; it's the absence of tropes.

I do these things in the place my grandfather had to leave to live life as a man. I do these things in a place that did not see my grandmother as beautiful. I do these things in a place that informs who I am. My children will know swamps and mountains firsthand. They will be raised as a part of nature. Entitled to. Beholden to.

I choose to live with the natural world, not separate from or exploited within. I choose to view my tactile relationship with the woods and the water as a satiating thing. It allows me space to change and mature. Always work, but never toil. The effort expands my capacity to be.

> Jonathan Wilkins is the founder of the Black Duck Revival, an organization that offers classes and experiences for hunters, anglers, birders, and artisans to learn and engage with the natural world in the Arkansas Delta region.

Detroit Hives

Timothy Paule and Nicole Lindsey

We find joy in being change agents for our community. Too many times development or change in our community is in the hands of someone, somewhere in a city office. So it brings us joy to be able to create the change that we want to see. We also find joy in being able to inspire the next generation of leaders in sustainability.

We both have a professional background in a variety of fields, but we wanted to do something together that allowed us to leverage all of our work experiences and community service. That's how we came up with the idea of trying to make a difference using vacant lots in Detroit. When a call to action from the City of Detroit asked residents to help transform the ninety thousand vacant lots in the city, we had a lot of ideas, but we didn't settle on one until after an illness that taught us about the powers of local honey. That's when Nicole had the idea of turning a vacant lot into a beehive.

In the beginning, a lot of our community thought we were crazy to become urban beekeepers. It wasn't until we personally invited them to come out and see how we were tending the bees that they saw how interesting it was. From these experiences, people come away knowing the difference between a honeybee and a yellow jacket, and then pass on that education to a friend or family member who might not have known. Giving people an

opportunity to learn about bees that is also welcoming and inviting to our culture and background is so inspiring and necessary.

A lot of people are afraid of bees and pollinator insects, or any type of creepy crawly insect. Sometimes the fears are inherited from our parents, or based on how insects are portrayed in the media, as pests and a nuisance that needs to stay away from humans. We get to teach the next generation that these pollinators are really important to our environment and that there's nothing to be afraid of. It brings joy to share a type of skill set and knowledge that wasn't passed down to us growing up. And to open up the eyes and minds of our youth to explore what's outside.

Little kids are usually enthused about learning, but a lot of teenagers or high school students can be timid at first. Once we give them a hands-on chance to assist, they are quickly engaged.

We have seen this shift with our niece. We introduced her to beekeeping at a young age, so she doesn't have that same fear of bees that we had growing up, seeing adults wave away or swat insects. Our niece is not afraid of bees because she knows that we are beekeepers. When she sees bees on flowers or a bee flying around her, she can even spot the distinct worker bee. She also knows that a bee landing on her means it thinks she's a flower— or looks or smells like one! A honeybee is not landing on you to cause harm, but instead to give a gift.

Bees teach us that honey is money, like health is wealth. It's a good lesson for humans. Imagine falling on hard times, maybe a financial crisis. How would you take care of yourself? You might do whatever it takes to provide for your family, but if you'd practiced good financial management, like honey management, you could have wealth stored up for you and even for the next generation. And that's exactly what honeybees do. They produce more honey than they will need in their lifetime of only four to six weeks, and that honey is available for the next generation. Honey is money. And when you store up that money like honey, you're not going to be as stressed out.

Honey is versatile and can do many things. It's healthy for you. It won't go bad, as long as you keep it sealed. It's antifungal and antibacterial. It's a great sweetener that won't spike your blood sugar. Honey lasts a lifetime, and you should have it with you all the time to heal both the inside and outside of the body.

All of this comes back to nature. You can't consume honey without thinking about nature. You can't put honey on your toast in the morning without thinking about the outdoors—without thinking about bees as pollinators. We live in a fast-paced world and bees help to remind us to appreciate the process that leads to harvest. Within a jar of honey that takes a whole season to harvest, each teaspoon requires so many miles of honeybee travel. Honey allows you to appreciate the time and energy required to make good food.

Bees have taught us so much. When we first began this work, we didn't know anything about beekeeping, and we asked ourselves, are we sure we want to do this? But together we saw the vision, and when you share a project together, it gives you both support and accountability. Teaching people about honeybees helps us see how fear is transformed into love.

We are in love with what we're doing. And together we enjoy spreading that love and impact in our community.

Timothy Paule and Nicole Lindsey are the founders of Detroit Hives. The couple established the organization to create sustainable communities and bee populations by transforming vacant lots into pollinator-friendly spaces. They are based in Detroit, Michigan.

Blood on My Hands

J. Drew Lanham

Watching birds. Hunting white-tailed deer. Wandering in wildness. Being the feral creature I am.

Hunting.

It is not a sport, or sporting. It is not a game, and I will not insult those wild things I seek by saying such. I have the overwhelmingly unfair advantage of technology, yet lose more than ninety-nine percent of the time, by my calculations. White-tailed deer's superior senses allow them to register shapes on the dim edges of night and day, making my own senses seem dull in comparison.

Evolution wins.

My calculations of what a white-tailed buck will do are really guesses. When I fail, I welcome the learning. The next guesses are marginally better, but then I may or may not pull the trigger or let loose the release. It is much more than a hobby to me. It is a life-and-death choice.

I never take lightly ending the life of another being. If ever I do, I'll stop. Yes, the intentions are often deadly. Lives are at stake. It is a reminder of the thin line we trod by flat foot or sharp hoof. If something dies by my hands, I have killed it. Not "harvested" it. There are no such things as wild, four-legged crops to pick! I'd rather know my meat blinked, bleated, and bounded free in wildness than stood knee-deep in its own waste. I'd rather know that some skill of accuracy I practiced on the shooting range delivers quick death rather than industrial slaughter, the kill hammer, and a disassembly line of ill-paid Brown people not given the respect of citizenship. The blood I willingly put on my hands is the price paid in white-tail sacrifice. One day I pray my ashes scattered on the wind will grow oaks and acorns and that the progeny of some deer that gave itself to me on a November morning will feast on what I once was.

Yes, I hunt. And I gather. I gather pieces of day, hermit thrush skulks and winter wren scurries. Count deceptive squirrels by the dozens. I marvel at a red fox's stealth as it moves silently over a forest floor of crisp, fallen leaves. I breathe better out here, high up in the tree stand. Life likely won't be choked out of me up here, either by virulent plague or by those who have no desire to serve or protect me. I feel safe. Secure. The constant reward is time away to consider these things. I sit. Think. Wonder. Watch. Occasionally—rarely—the result is venison. Mostly, it is just me with life on a different plane to consider. Climbing high to look out. It is why I hunt.

Love of nature is love of self. That's where all healing and joy begin: within.

J. Drew Lanham is the author of *The Home Place: Memoirs of a Colored Man's Love Affair with Nature*, which received the Reed Award from the Southern Environmental Law Center and the Southern Book Prize, and was a finalist for the John Burroughs Medal. He is a birder, naturalist, and hunter-conservationist who has published essays and poetry in numerous publications.

In the Name of Joy

Nature as a Healer

The first time I consciously connected with the power of the natural world I was a young child. It was a warm autumn afternoon on our Lake County ranch at the end of a full weekend of visiting family and friends, so typical at our summer home. I had spent the entire day in the pool until the skin on the tips of my fingers and toes pruned. I was walking around the entire length of the pool, passing the forbidden *deep end,* when a form at my feet caught my eye: glistening brown leaves moistened by water lay pressed flat into the wet concrete. Peach tree leaves that had already come loose in the fall warmth.

I stopped and asked out loud to those leaves, "What do you know?"

I don't recall their answer, but that was my first memory of consciously connecting with, and asking something from, the natural world, guided by an intuition there might be an answer. A problem that could be solved. In my work leading Outdoor Afro, I've discovered that I can unlock that same intuition to connect with nature to find answers and solve problems.

In 2014, America's cities erupted in response to yet another police-involved death of a Black person, this time in Ferguson, Missouri. At that time, the Outdoor Afro office operated from a stylish, community-centered co-working space in uptown Oakland, near the epicenter of our city. As I left the office, I felt a thick tension in the air on that warm autumn weekday afternoon. I walked through the concrete parking lot to my car, and I could hear the distinct rumble of helicopters, along with a distant sighing screech, as electric saws cut plywood to be hammered over street-facing store windows. Growing up in Oakland, I had seen this before. Felt this before. An urgent civic brace to prepare for unrest.

I was feeling angry and hurt, too, as a mother of two Black sons. As I'd taken in the news, I felt an incredible weight, combined with feelings of empathy for the lives senselessly lost, for all the connected kin, and a generational ache, remembering the souls of Emmett Till and countless others similarly sentenced to death.

Walking across that uptown Oakland concrete to my car, I asked myself, as a Black woman leading a Black-focused organization, "What should *I* do? What do *I* know?"

This time the answer came. Clearly.

"You do *nature*, Rue—that's *your* lane."

So I spent the next few days calling my friends and Outdoor Afro partners to talk through all our complex emotions at that moment, then I asked each one to join me in solidarity for that weekend in my favorite biome—the redwoods—for what would become the first Outdoor Afro Healing Hike.

I did not think through what a Healing Hike was supposed to be about, but I knew instinctively, like I did when I was a little girl looking at those wet leaves on the ground, that the redwoods in my hometown Oakland's hills—where I had played as a child, found love, and experienced my own adult healing—might hold an answer.

The following Saturday, about thirty strangers assembled around those redwoods. Although we were an almost all-Black participant group, we did not share the same viewpoints, and we were of different generations; yet I felt we all instinctively recognized we needed to find a safe way to find healing.

Among those redwood trees, there were no helicopters overhead. No sounds of plywood hammering into place. And no police in riot gear. All we had was one another and those trees. Those third-generation redwoods

"As we walked, I could feel the tension sliding off our shoulders, giving way to easy laughter, deep sighs of relief, and backslapping encouragement. In that moment, under the gaze of the trees, we were united in our humanity. We were the same."

that sprang from a clear-cut past had witnessed much in their 150 years, and they were surely able to absorb our moment.

We convened in a meadow to set our intentions as a group, and my dear friend Nikki Thomas, a community yoga instructor, led us in breathing and stretching to anchor our group with intention for who we wanted to be in that moment. Then we filed out with soft, purposeful steps to begin our hike. As we walked, I could feel the tension sliding off our shoulders, giving way to easy laughter, deep sighs of relief, and backslapping encouragement. In that moment, under the gaze of the trees, we were united in our humanity. We were the same.

Our trail eventually led us to a creek in a valley of redwoods, where we took a moment to share reflections and commitments for what we might do and be for our communities once we emerged from those redwoods.

I will get the youth together in our community and educate them on our history.

I will come back here when I am feeling overwhelmed.

I will pass on the baton and wisdom of what activism means.

In that moment I realized that our group was doing what Black people have always known we could do: lay our burdens—in the lyrics of our ancestors—*down by the riverside.* Like them, we found hope and a way to break through to our freedom.

That was the day I clearly understood the value of nature as a healer, and recognized my responsibility to continue to lift up this value. And ever since, my organization has been turning to nature to heal and teach with intention. It has now become a part of the way we train our organization's volunteer leaders, and has reinforced my own practice to turn to nature in times of need.

Writer Paulo Coelho says it best in his book *By the River Piedra I Sat Down and Wept:* "Joy is sometimes a blessing, but it is often a conquest." This passage has been an inspiration for me, as it reminds me that nature is a source of peace and healing, and therefore a bridge to lasting joy.

In the contributions that follow, you will witness journeys of pain that metamorphosize beautifully into healing and joy, as Akiima Price's portrait "Nature's Healing

Frequency" describes how nature can help stressed communities access liberation; alongside revelations of connectivity and triumph that root us in our passion and personal purpose, as Jason Swann describes in "Colorado: A True Love Story"; and as you will read in Alora Jone's kaleidoscope vision, "Raindrops and Fireflies," where she finds love.

This is *exactly* what I have always hoped my work could demonstrate: a possibility for both transformational healing and joy for everyone.

—Rue

Colorado: A True Love Story

Jason Swann

I've climbed mountains so high above the clouds that heaven's gates seemed only a staircase away. I've slept under the glistening petals of the Milky Way and woke to the horizon of God's fiery blaze—a reminder that darkness is impermanent. I've learned to speak the language of the earth through the soles of my feet. Journeyed for hundreds of miles to be closer to her equanimity, her enormity of care, her fortress of solitude. I've met explorers, farmers, ranchers, hunters and anglers, environmental activists, and outdoor enthusiasts. But *never* have I met a love so potent, so forgiving and unscathed, righteous and true. Though I'll be gone, I won't forget you, Colorado, my first love and my forever dream come true.

Jason Swann is an advocate for equitable access to public open spaces. He is the founder of Rising Routes, an organization committed to social justice, environmental stewardship, and mental wellness. Jason is based in Colorado.

Nature's Healing Frequency

Akiima Price

Growing up in the '70s and '80s, I saw the crack epidemic firsthand. I asked myself as a teen, "What could I bring to the world that could make it better for my people?" I knew I could not fix racism, but that I could do individual things in my sphere of influence. I just had to figure out what those were.

I ultimately discovered the power of nature in helping people heal. And that brings me joy to witness it every day in my life's work. Early in my career in the environmental field I was always assigned to work with stressed Black American communities that were considered "hard to reach." I did not mind because these audiences were familiar to me and inspired me to be creative in making environmental concepts understandable. I was successful, but the organizations never respected my recipe, which included more of a focus on effective outcomes than cognitive outcomes. These children were living in situations that would break the average human, and while they were super smart and resilient, they were often labeled "bad." But I saw a difference in them when they were given a chance to be outside, to have access to a field to run through, to experience live animals, to have the opportunity to care for something. Witnessing that validated my belief in the power of nature and encouraged my career path in nontraditional environmental education.

Nature is not like a test you can pass or fail. It is a liberation that comes from the comfort and safety of being in an organic space. The birds that fly over your head and catch your attention. The smell of the flowers can take you away.

The people that I've seen in my work, as a nature-based programming specialist, are most often folks who come from very stressed communities. And I witness them become childlike in nature and rediscover their innocence again. That is the work that brings me joy, because nature does the same for me.

There's something about when I'm in a natural environment—I know it's bigger than me. In nature I find a frequency that matches the frequency that lives under my anger, my frustration, and my stress. And as the volume of my nature turns up, like the clarity that comes through the frequency of a song, that moment of stress I might find myself in burns away, and reminds me of how much bigger nature is than whatever I might face in my life.

Akiima currently resides in her hometown of Washington, D.C., not far from the eastern shore of Maryland, where she prefers to spend most of her free time, surrounded by nature and water. Her inherent appreciation of the restorative value of nature informs her efforts to build and promote meaningful outdoor engagement in marginalized communities.

The Art of Bird Dogs

Durrell Smith

I enjoy research. I enjoy history. I enjoy bird dogs. That is where my joy starts.

I got into bird dogs—dogs that are bred and trained to find game—several years ago. Around that time I serendipitously stumbled across images of Neal Carter and Curtis Brooks, Black bird dog experts, in *Garden and Gun* magazine. In the photos they had these two beautiful white pointers posed up on the back of a tailgate. At that moment it was like looking at a picture of Michael Jordan or LeBron James—I was like, man, I want to do *that*.

I made it my pursuit to meet Carter and Brooks. I found that they were from South Georgia, and I was familiar with the area because I'd gone to school at Albany State University.

That was the beginning of my Black joy in the natural world. Now I enjoy seeing stark-white, long-tailed English pointers run through the piney woods, locked up on point. Then we go in and flush a covey of quail, and they get on up and you fire your gun, though most of the time it's a blank pistol, so there is seldom any pressure to kill.

Everybody can tell you that the South is super spiritual. I grew up Southern Baptist—you know how Black folks are about religion, like that's where we get a lot of our strength and that's where we find solace. The piney woods of South Georgia offer that to me. Getting out there working my dogs every

day helps me take my mind off everything negative that's going on in the world. Working with bird dogs is an art form, and I'm an artist. Everything that they do came off my creative hand.

My research on Neal Carter and Curtis Brooks taught me the long-standing history of bird dogs that defies most people's understanding of what Black folks are capable of. We've been practicing this art for generations, and that history was never written down. So now I'm writing it down as my contribution to bird dog history. Imagine how good you have to be to not only transcend the circumstances of the South and its past history, but also keep a hold on that methodology and that art form, constantly refine it over the years, and then pass it on to the next generation of young Black folks. Discovering this history was so *dope* to me. Today I use all this knowledge as I guide hunts. I especially love when people come from out of town; I get them connected with the mythology and the ethos of quail hunting in the South. And then I'm able to show them based on an age-old art form that came from Black folks. It's all cyclical.

> Durrell Smith lives in Atlanta, Georgia. He and his wife are founders of the Minority Outdoors Alliance, an organization that encourages people of color to embrace the great outdoors.

The Breath of a Summit

Shane Douglas

The area where I grew up, Broadleaf Circle, is an idyllic neighborhood in a quiet corner of a quiet suburb, with a neat row of low-slung two-story homes on the outer circle and a well-manicured park area that fills the inner space inside the road. One day, my mom and I made the short journey from our home to the grassy, open space in the center of the circle. As she approached the top of a small mound, she glanced over her shoulder to find me lagging behind and gasping for breath. This gentle, rolling hill shouldn't cause anyone to struggle breathing, and especially not an active elementary schooler who hadn't even started running around.

I don't remember walking with Mom or gasping for air, nor do I remember visiting the doctor the next day and being diagnosed with asthma. I do, however, have a faint recollection of my parents' relief at the moderate diagnosis, especially once we filled the prescription for a series of inhalers that were to become my daily companion over the next decade. The panicked gasping and struggling to gather enough precious oxygen to breathe became nothing more than a distant memory as I outgrew my asthmatic symptoms in one of the few positive changes that puberty and teenage years provided.

Years later, I'm hurtling down a narrow trail. I no longer hear the sound of my sneakers pounding against the smooth dirt trail. Or the branches whipping back into place after my arms or thighs or shins pull them forward with my momentum. I can no longer make out the soft sound of the small creek below, winding and tracking the curves of the path. All I can hear is the sound of my heart throbbing in my ears, and in the brief moments between beats, I notice my blood pulsating as it carries oxygen to the various parts of my body.

Thump thump whoosh, thump thump whoosh, thump thump whoosh. I'm used to the sound of my heartbeat, yet the soundtrack of my blood seems alien in my ears. Over the past couple minutes, an urge, which began timidly and quietly, has erupted into a full-throated roar. I don't know what's behind me, but I can sense that something's there. I want to look over my shoulder. I need to look over my shoulder. But if I do, even for a brief second, I will slow the pace, and that's simply not an option when running in a marathon.

Desperate for distraction, I hone my precision on the accuracy of my foot placement. My body moves more rapidly through the dense forest and my eyes adapt to this new speed. A paler, lighter brown might just be a change in the dirt or could be a gnarled root lying in wait to catch my toe. Rutted-out terrain bobs and weaves on the edge of the trail with no obvious pattern. The chaos makes it impossible to predict what comes next. My intense examination of the pounded path has another benefit beyond distracting me from the activity itself: I become more aware of my breath. With each deep inhalation, I appreciate that I'm able to bring the hot, damp air into my body when I need it the most.

Only as I come around the last tight corner do my pupils begin to constrict to prepare for the flood of sunshine. I widen my stride as the path expands. There are no more roots to trip me—at least not today. And while my heart continues to dominate and overwhelm all other sounds, I'm able to breathe freely, easily, and without obstruction or friction.

The winding trail spits me out of the thick, tangled grove of trees into the blaring August sun. The uncomfortably bright light takes a few moments to adjust to, as does the shifting and undulating of the gravel under my feet. I'd grown accustomed to the well-worn dirt track during my marathon. While it contained traps and obstacles around every corner, at least there was consistency.

My fingers instinctively clasp together as I raise my hands and open up my chest. I'd stop, but I have far too much momentum to stand in place, and as I impatiently wait for my heart to quiet down, my gaze turns up toward an imposing, impressive ridge that dominates my view. Staring up at the mountain reminds me of how far I've come from trying to summit the tiny mound years before.

Shane Douglas works to leverage technology platforms for social impact, and serves on a number of nonprofits boards and advisory groups. He resides in Washington D.C. with his wife and child.

That Is in Us

Faith E. Briggs

"No one is hot, not even me,

under the shade of my calabash tree.

No one is hot, not even me,

under the shade of my calabash tree."

I made up this song when I was six. Perhaps it was inspired by the lyrical Anansi the Spider stories I read around that time—stories where I first heard of a calabash. Those tales spoke to me, and I was inspired to make up my own new songs and stories, as I ran around barefoot in wet grass as a kid. I'd find a big branch downed from an East Coast summer thunderstorm, and parade around singing to myself with the branch propped over my shoulder.

When I can find that little girl, that creative little child who spent a lot of time on her own, making up worlds, inspired by everything she saw around her, I am at my happiest. I think that is also when I am at my best. It fuels me, that feeling, and the desire to share it.

Now that I am grown, spending time outside is not so much about creating a relationship with the outdoors. It's reconnecting with the mud and the sunshine and the creeks that I knew growing up.

And I know not everyone grew up that way, especially many people of color. At the same time, I also know that we've been fed lies about ourselves for so long, it's sometimes hard to disprove the myths, even to ourselves.

There is a myth that says that Black people don't have a relationship with the natural world. The image that has been popularized in the American imagination is of city-dwelling people who only know and love concrete and bricks. I think our ability to so fully adapt to any environment, to the point that we make it ours, is a testament to our resilience. We thrived culturally, even when given the most unwanted places and things.

That's one of the things I love about being Black.

The truth is that we built this country. We worked its soil. We introduced our crops, from seeds braided into our hair when we were stolen across the seas. We made Sunday gardens and bought our bodies back by selling the additional vegetables that we could grow on our own, despite being enslaved. And when we were free, we remained the knowledge keepers of the earth. Our knowledge was so valuable that new insidious methods of tying us to the economy were created: sharecropping, debt peonage. We had to steal away in the night to go North, even as "free" people. In so many cases, we were forced to leave the land to try to get free. In so many cases, the land was taken from us, by force and violence and cheating.

We took with us so much knowing. It is in our grandmother's hands, in our cooking, in our windowsill gardens. It is in us. It's been there for generations, epigenetic. The feeling of a cool breeze on our necks, warm mud under our feet, the in-between moments of the taste of freedom on the wind, of singing together outside. That is in us.

If you open up a page of any Toni Morrison book, nature is present. Try it.

I learned about how I can be a cool Baptist from Morrison. I learned about quiet forest clearings and the taste of soil and salt from Toni Cade Bambara. I learned about great floods, wishes traveling on the sea, and the light at daybreak from Zora Neale Hurston. I learned about the softness of the wind and the lightness of the dew from Audre Lorde. When I wade into the water to fish, as I cast I think of Langston Hughes, telling me that I have known rivers.

So I know that the time I spend outside, interacting with and learning from the natural world, is my legacy. It brings me such joy to know it. To be reminded of it. And to remind others. This is a reclamation.

When I walk outside, I think the trees smile to see me there.

I feel like they welcome me and know me.

And I know them.

Faith E. Briggs is a documentary filmmaker, creative producer, director, writer, and podcast host passionate about sharing contemporary stories from diverse communities. She is based in Portland Oregon.

Joy Is a Revelation

Carolyn Finney

In the fall of 2001, I dug my backpack out of my closet and prepared to travel from New York City to Nepal to spend a year as a Fulbright scholar. I was no stranger to the Himalayas; I had lived in Nepal before, so it was like preparing to reconnect with an old friend. But this time was different. When the Towers fell on 9/11 my heart was crushed along with the many souls who died that day. I found it hard to find joy in leaving New York, the place of my birth. I found it hard to leave my family when my father had recently revealed he was battling prostate cancer. I found it hard to see or feel or breathe or dream.

But I got on the plane with my backpack, my hiking boots, and my tired heart. I was just going through the motions of living and was grateful that I had a plan in place once I arrived in Kathmandu: I was going to hike the Annapurna Conservation Area with my friend Ellen, an accomplished cellist who was flying over just for this purpose. The trek takes about three weeks to hike, following a horseshoe loop of the national park with trails as high as 17,000 feet. We hired a local Nepali guide whose knowledge, skill, and generosity of spirit made it possible for me to relinquish any sense or pretense that I was in control of (or even cared about) the journey we were embarking upon.

Each day started around 6:00 a.m. Ellen and I shared a room in local lodges, which usually consisted of simple bedrooms, a common eating area, and

a shared outhouse for all guests. Our alarm clock would go off—we'd be on opposite sides of the room in our respective beds—and I'd look over at Ellen, who always seemed to get up with a smile on her face. I would reluctantly sit up in my sleeping bag, put my head in my hands, and say, "Oh crap—another day." We'd grab something to eat with our Nepali guide, put our backpacks on our backs, and begin what would be anywhere from a six- to eight-hour hike to the next place we would spend the night.

Trails were diverse, unique, and particular, and we adjusted our gait and pace accordingly. Sometimes I was scared—the trail would be so narrow and the drop-off so steep that injury or death felt imminent. There was no room for emotional self-indulgence or living in the past. "Be here now," the mountains whispered. The flora changed all the time. The colors and smells coaxed me out of my darkness as my blistered feet kept moving through the pain. I found myself looking forward to our daily lunch break of *dal baht* (lentils and rice), which we would devour with the sun on our faces while being assaulted by an outrageously gorgeous view in every direction.

Over the course of those weeks and miles, a profound shift took place within me. On the last day of the trek, my clothes dirty, my feet sore, and dreams of a hot shower about to be realized, I found myself upright once more. I found myself alive in the fullest sense. I found myself grateful for the time with my friend. I found myself humbled by the nature around me. I found that I could see and feel and dream. I found that my heart could still sing.

Joy is a multidimensional feeling that expands and contracts as it responds to pain, emerges in healing, and is expressed in the day-to-day experience of being in relationship to our world. That three-week trek through the mountains brought me to myself: the crispness of the air and a sky so close and so blue, I thought it would break my heart with its beauty; the feel of the ground beneath my feet as each step took me higher, deeper, and closer to life as we know it with all its pleasure, pain, and mystery; the gift of memory and laughter when I reflect back on my own resistance to healing revealed in how I started each day. The mountains knew. And even when I lay on the side of the trail, altitude sickness robbing me of my ability to fully breathe at 16,000 feet, the ground held me. My friend held me. The sky held me.

Joy is a revelation—a revealing of the boundlessness of our hearts and its capacity to heal. Nature speaks all languages and breathes for us every day, even when we've forgotten how to. We are connected to everything. The mountains did not judge and the trail brought me home.

Carolyn Finney, PhD, is a storyteller, writer, and cultural geographer who works at the intersection of the arts, education, and lived experience. She is the author of *Black Faces, White Spaces: Reimagining the Relationship of African Americans to the Great Outdoors.*

Learning to Swim

Bryson Sutton

My name is Bryson and I am ten years old. I love the outdoors and I am now learning how to swim. I really wanted to learn after going whitewater rafting for the first time with my mom. I had never been on a river before. After we rafted, there was a swimming pool near where we camped. I saw all the other kids swimming, but I still needed a lifejacket. I told my mom I wanted to learn to swim too.

I have been learning for a while now. I can hold my breath underwater for fifteen seconds. I can freestyle, backstroke, and tread water. Now, when I get to go on whitewater raft trips, I can swim with the other kids in the camp pool.

I think I want to join a swim team one day, but right now, I like seeing birds come to our bird feeder for a chat, and riding on the marina with my mom and dad in the summer.

> Bryson Sutton is an elementary school student who enjoys reading, sports, and celebrations with his family.

Black Girls Climb Trees

Jilchristina Vest

When I was ten years old I was struck by lightning. It was the late 1970s, and my sister, Julia, and I were deep into our Chicago backyard's giant oak tree, perched high for the best view of the storm going on around us. *Crack* went the lightning, then the count "one, two, three, four, five. . ." until *Boom* came the thunder. The shorter the count between the lightning and thunder, the more excited we would get.

Our grandfather saw us from the upstairs window and told us to get out of that tree immediately and get back in the house before we were struck by lightning. We were not children who had to be told something twice. We immediately started to scramble our way down the branches to the ladder. And it was then, when we were halfway down the ladder, that we saw and felt the lightning strike the ground beneath the aluminum ladder. I remember it like a cartoon. Once the electricity was gone and we were able to move we got into the house and ran into the basement. We thought one of two things: either we were dead and were therefore gonna get in a lot of trouble, or we now had superpowers. Welp. The only part that came true was the trouble.

I'm still that little Black girl who grew up outside. I'm fifty-four years old, and whenever I see a tree I think about whether or not it would be a good

one to climb. When I see an anthill I think about lying on my belly to get a closer look at them going to and fro, carrying their wares, carrying their food, caring for one another. When it's hot I give fire hydrants the side eye, close my eyes, and smile from ear to ear. So much joy in these memories.

I grew up in Chicago and Battle Creek, Michigan, running through fire hydrants in the city and swimming at Goguac Lake in Michigan. Spending summers fishing with my grandpa at Green Lake and camping Zion Park outside of Chicago, learning how to start a fire, clean a fish, and go to the bathroom in the woods. Being outside is what we did, squealing as we jumped off piers or out of trees, as we chased ice cream trucks and fireflies, or built snowballs, snow people, and snow tunnels. It was all joy.

No adventure was off the table—like when my father decided that we were going to be skiers. We drove to Wisconsin and took downhill lessons, but it turned out I was terrified of heights and refused to jump off the ski lift when it got to the top. I took it all the way back down and I jumped off and said "Nope." That same day I discovered cross-country skiing. This was another moment of Black joy outside, refusing to go inside and instead finding something new about myself as a little girl. Because as long as I was outside, I was happy.

Nowadays I don't search for snow; I search for turquoise water and white sand and to be surrounded by people who look like me. I want to be near or in the ocean, be warm and calm and quiet.

As I have grown up, what I like most when I travel is seeing other Black people taking up space, enjoying the outdoors, enjoying the earth and new places. I travel a lot by myself. It's that glance, that smile when you meet the eyes of somebody else that you know might be a Black American. It happens everywhere: Paris, Tokyo, Johannesburg, Cartagena. That smile and that glance of recognition is something that always brings me joy and makes me smile.

I am most peaceful floating on my back in the ocean, relaxing my head in the water, and the sound that comes with it. I look up at the sky and I don't hear or see any people. Just me, the powerful Yoruba goddess, Yemayah, and the sun. When I hear the ocean, my eyes close and my smile broadens. It is my purest form of joy. That little Black girl with lightning-given super-powers, outdoors, in the sun.

Jilchristina Vest is the curator of the West Oakland Mural Project. Inspired by the art that emerged during the uprisings for Black lives in 2020, Jilchristina organized the first-ever public art installation honoring the women of the Black Panther Party and the #SayHerName movement. She is based in Oakland, California.

Raindrops and Fireflies

Alora Jones

I am sitting under nature's umbrella in front of this cracking fire, as raindrops fall and sizzle in the flames. Feet wet and heart full, I can't help but quietly celebrate this confluence of two great loves.

Two years ago, you would not have made it to this campsite with me. Now look at you, raindrops in your 'fro and a grin on your face. You look at me like there's no place in the world you'd rather be, and I wholeheartedly agree. I thank my lucky stars for the transformational powers of nature and love.

Our paths might never have crossed at all. Yet here I find myself, strolling arm-in-arm along this dark trail with you to the most spectacular light show on Earth. The river serenades us as the forest glimmers and flickers to its song. Who could be more perfect to share this moment with than the love who makes me feel like this all the time?

So, to the man who always puts fireflies in my belly, this is what it feels like to be loved by you: It's the wonder when you first notice the star inside of a cottonwood twig. A snowflake landing gently on your eyelash, offering a fresh perspective of winter. It's finally reaching your summit and having that moment to just breathe. It's that swagger in the way you lean back while you steer our canoe. It's defying the elements and building a roaring fire anyway, raindrop sizzles and all. It's . . . everything, my darling.

And I'm so grateful you chose me to go on this adventure with you.

> Alora Jones is a outdoor recreation enthusiast who leads members of her community on excursions into Minnesota parks.

Wild Healing

Rae Wynn-Grant

Nature came to my rescue more than a decade ago, when I was recovering from a very debilitating emotional smackdown. Earlier that year, I'd taken my abuser (a young white man of privilege) to court on very serious charges, and the judge sided with his word over mine. I was devastated, humiliated, and regretful that I had even tried to use the legal system to protect me in the first place. It was an extremely traumatic process that ended with my story ultimately not being believed.

Despite the overwhelming mental toll this experience took on me, I remained an active, engaged, and high-achieving graduate student who hid my pain and depression quite well. I often found beautiful escapes in my wildlife ecology studies in the classroom, so developing a summer research experience rooted in this work was a joy. With an undergraduate study-abroad experience in East Africa studying wildlife conservation behind me, I developed an independent research project on human–lion conflict in Central Tanzania that would become my master's thesis work. I applied for grants, arranged fieldwork permits and intern status at a major wildlife conservation nonprofit, and set off to the Tanzanian bush for a summer largely by myself.

The life-changing experiences I had while sleeping in a tent in the Tanzanian wilderness for three months tracking lions by day, dodging water-raiding elephants by night, and exploring the gorgeous East African savannas were

too numerous to count. But what still brings me such a sense of gratitude is how emotionally healed I was when I returned to my university life in the United States after my summer in the wild. From spending hours a day observing the behaviors of female lions running their prides, to learning to harvest medicinal plants with the Maasai warriors who protected me and served as my guides, to sleeping in the outdoors under the stars at one with nature on the continent that birthed my ancestors, slowly but surely I found rest, inner peace, and renewed self-confidence. My healing was directly facilitated by nature, and although these days I don't anticipate spending three months away in the wilderness without anyone I know, I have the memories. It was more powerful than any experience I've had since.

Today, my time in nature is abundant because of my career. I am now a wildlife ecologist who collects data on wild animal movement and behavior by engaging in very active field-based science, which often involves handling wild animals. Because of this, I'm most often spending time in nature for professional, rather than recreational, reasons. And yet the particular role I play in nature as a scientist on a mission for discovery allows me to be challenged in so many different ways, and to grow, learn, and deepen during each experience. I often go looking for things that I don't end up finding. For example, my task is often to find a bear or evidence of a bear's presence in a certain landscape. I may spend days, weeks, or even months looking for the animal, or paw prints, claw marks, dens, or even poop! And many times, despite my efforts, I come up empty-handed. This is when I grow the most.

With Mother Earth under my feet, and clear sky over my head, and living, breathing, vibrant wilderness all around me, I challenge myself to feel not defeated, but rather embraced. I challenge myself to accept that many animals don't want to be found, and that scientific discovery can also occur in the absence of an animal. I challenge myself to acknowledge my effort, no matter the outcome. And more than anything, I challenge myself to enjoy my company—to love myself when I'm dirty, tired, lost, or failing. These wonderful moments occur often enough that when I gear up to head into the field, I find myself curiously contemplating what inward discovery I'll come back with this time.

Rae Wynn-Grant is a large carnivore ecologist and a fellow with National Geographic Society; she is best known for her research on the human impact on the behavior of black bears in Montana. She is an advocate for women and people of color in the sciences.

Joy Journey

Angelou Ezeilo

The outdoors. Nature. The environment. Outside. These terms mean so many different things to different people depending on where you live, what you look like, and perhaps how much money is in your bank account. For me, a fifty-year-old African American woman, they all mean freedom.

But my relationship with the outdoors is complicated.

When I was a little girl and was told to go outside and play, nothing made me happier. My friends were outside, I could play double Dutch there, my favorite park was there, and most of all I could be and do whatever I wanted there. It was amazing.

I wanted this same love affair that I had with the outdoors for every child, which led me to the work that I do today with Greening Youth Foundation. However, working over the past two decades to ensure equity for people of color in the environmental sector has taken a personal toll on me. You see, because I am an empathic person, it physically pains me to know that there are children who don't have access to the beauty and healing powers of nature. All children need this. But given the oppressive history of this country as it relates to people of color, many Black and Brown children do not have equitable access.

As I have been relentlessly working on this matter for so long, it is hard for me to go out and enjoy nature without thinking about the layers of complexities surrounding it. When I go for a hike in a park, I think, Why are there no other Black people in this park right now? Or, when I visit public lands, I find myself thinking, Have Native Americans been considered/included in the creation of this park/forest/refuge? It's hard for my mind to stop. At times the only way I can turn off my brain and stop analyzing the situation is to leave.

But to preserve my own well-being, I need to recapture the carefree relationship I had with nature as a child.

I want my joy back!

Hiking . . .

Bird watching . . .

Star gazing . . .

Jumping rope . . .

Biking . . .

Fishing . . .

I am on a journey to reclaim the joyful relationship I have with nature. And I am starting right now.

Angelou Ezeilo is a social entrepreneur and environmental activist. She is the founder of Greening Youth Foundation, an international nonprofit that was created to engage underrepresented youth and young adults while connecting them to the outdoors and careers in conservation. She currently lives in Atlanta with her husband.

ACKNOWLEDGMENTS

There is not a day that goes by that I don't feel the touch of grace and gratitude for my mother, Willie Bell Montgomery, known fondly as Alice. I am so thankful for being your do-over, and I hope I've made you proud.

For the entire Levias family, especially for the care and deep American South culture gifted to me by both my father, A.C. and his wife, Ella mae, who raised me. Each one paved the way for the hospitality and joy in community nature experiences that sit at the heart of all I do—and now, at the center of this book.

Sister Delane is a guardian angel to many, but especially to me as a lifeline for love, generational understanding, and support; at many critical turning points in my journey, she has made the difference.

My beautiful and brilliant children—Seth, Arwen, and Billy: You have each given me so much through the miracle of motherhood and most especially for all you have done to teach me the joy of parenting in nature. I appreciate the sacrifices you made missing your momma while I pursued education and an ambitious career. I hope you realize how important you are in this journey and what it means for the world, and my love for you always.

Darin, I am so thankful for the love and support you share so generously. You are my best friend, my rock of reason, and now a permanent blind partner! I thank my lucky stars we found each other again after so many years. Now it's me and you 'til the end, baby!

For my Book Club Beauties (BCB)—Erica, Gina, Kara, Niambi, Nikki, and Talithia: Your friendship over the past four decades has been my daily joy and spiritual support through all of life's weather. And yes, we are more than books!

I'm thankful for the entire Outdoor Afro community, which has grown in both number and depth over the years and informs so much of what this book is about. I am especially grateful for the volunteers, staff, board members, creatives, and generous partners—supporters who have become lifelong friends, champions, and investors in my continued growth as a leader and human being. Shout out to REI, The Wilderness Society, The William and Flora Hewlett Foundation, The Pisces Foundation, KEEN, Klean Kanteen, and so many more from the outdoor industry—thanks to you all for being early believers and investors in me and my work. Beth Pratt, you always knew I had a book in me!

There is no way I would have been ready to actually sit down and *write* this book without the confidence and loving support that Roundtable Companies gave me. I am especially grateful for the joy of Kelsey Schurer, whose brilliance, warmth, and creativity helped me find and elevate my voice as an author. It is the gift that will continue to give. Thank you!

Big thanks to Maggie Cooper, my Aevitas Creative agent, who discovered me and has been a beacon of elevated possibility and sparkling intelligence as my guide, thought partner, and advocate. She helped me make a meaningful and visionary entry into the publishing world. With many moving parts to manage in my life, I could not have gotten this book over the finish line without my colleague Deborah Hayman. She rallied hard for so many elements of the book, and I am especially grateful for her cheerful support and can-do spirit, especially leading up to our important deadlines.

From the moment I first heard from Sahara Clement in the summer of 2020, the team at Chronicle Books proved that it *was* possible to create the book of my dreams, filled with beautiful images to celebrate Black joy. I'm ever grateful for the ways both Rachel Hiles and Becca Hunt shepherded me as guiding editors, championed the preservation of every voice, gave me gentle nudges on upcoming deadlines, and embodied faith and excitement for the vision and experience of writing this book.

I'm so grateful that book designer Maggie Edelman and photographer Bethanie Hines hiked with me and members of the community in the Oakland Hills redwoods to capture a beautiful, crisp visual story to inspire imagination and nourish the soul for readers of all ages.

Thanks also to the rest of the Chronicle team: Alison Throckmorton, Morgan Gutierrez, Heather Fisk, Natalie Nicolson, and April Whitney.

Nature Swagger is deeply enriched by the contributions of each individual you get to meet in this book. They each entrusted me with friendship and candid experiences. Together, we got to share a new, beautiful, and empowering representation of Black people in nature. Let's keep it going, please!

Adimika Arthur

Akiima Price

Alison Rose Jefferson

Alora Jones

Angelo Paez

Angelou Ezeilou

Antoine Skinner

Bryson Sutton

Camille Dungy

Carolyn Finney

Cordelia "Betty" Hinkson Brown

Dudley Edmondson

Durrell Smith

Elaine Lee

Evita Robinson

Faith E. Briggs

J. Drew Lanham

Jason Swann

Jilchristina Vest

Jonathan Wilkins

Julius Crowe Hampton

Leah Penniman

Leandra Taylor

Nicole Lindsey

Pandora Thomas

Phil Henderson

Rae Wynn-Grant

Rick Blocker

Robin Brumfield-Johnson

Shane Douglas

Shelton Johnson

Shonda Scott

Suzette Chang

Tamu Curtis

Taylor Nelson

Teralynn Nelson

Tiara Phalon

Timothy Paule

Virgil Baker

Yanira M. Castro

In God's Natural Grace,

Rue

ONWARD

I hope *Nature Swagger* has piqued your interest in exploring the wide variety of ways to enjoy nature. I realize it highlights only a small slice of the many stories and experiences that stand on the shoulders of generations past, but I hope it will inspire further learning and exploration in nature for everyone.

While this book certainly does not contain every possibility, location, or activity to enjoy in nature, it is my hope that it's left you yearning for more! I encourage you to turn to your own family and community history for stories of Black connections and joy in nature that you can record with photos, poems, and prose to share with generations to come.

If you are pioneering a new journey into the outdoors in your community, seek out the many groups, camps, clubs, outdoor retailers, and public park agencies that are waiting to welcome you to their programs or to offer tips and advice to help you feel confident and prepared for your next outdoor adventure.

I am thrilled that digital platforms remain a fruitful pathway for finding new activity partners. Affinity groups like Outdoor Afro will help you discover inspiring images and will invite you to join the ever-growing community of outdoor enthusiasts from every walk of life.

With your inspired love of and engagement with nature, together with the stories of *Nature Swagger*, we will achieve a new narrative in which connections in nature are an ordinary yet meaningful part of everyone's life.

CREDITS